JED TALKS #3

The Tao of the Large-Breasted
Goddess with the Shapely Behind

JED MCKENNA

Jed Talks #3

The Tao of the Large-Breasted
Goddess with the Shapely Behind

Jed McKenna

Print ISBN: 978-1-7343534-0-2
E-Book ISBN: 978-1-7343534-1-9

Contents

How could you rise anew if you
have not first become ashes?

Friedrich Nietzsche

I Am an Apple Tree

Show me a sane man
and I will cure him for you.

C. G. Jung

W E'RE SOMEWHERE IN THE MOUNTAINS, an hour by foot from home. I'm looking for a tennis ball on a rocky slope below the path from which I threw it. Maya, my sub-intrepid Border Collie, failed to do her one simple job and now sits safely on the path watching me play fetch. Slope-below-path here means rugged mountainside; steep, rock-strewn, viney, cluttered with rotted treefall and tangled underbrush into which no sane person would venture for love or money, much less a slobbery tennis ball. Sanity, how-ever, has never been one of my shortcomings.

1

I reflect briefly on the many hundreds of hours I've spent over the years kicking around in weeds and overgrown ditches or risking life and limb to find an unfetched tennis ball. Who's the dog in this scenario?

"She's making you her bitch," she says. Not the dog, obviously; dogs can't talk.

"Yeah, I get that," I say testily, straddling a ravine with slimy moss for a foothold. One slip and the next fifty feet will be gravity-fueled and very bumpy.

"Maybe throwing balls on a steep mountain path isn't the best idea," she says.

A word-sound from childhood almost escapes my lips. It would have sounded like this, *adoi-eee*, and would be meant to express sarcastic agreement with an over-obvious statement. I don't give it voice, but when conversing with her, unspoken doesn't mean unheard.

"Very mature," she says.

I see the ball. It's a dozen feet below me between some tumbled boulders. I can't get straight to it and going around to a safer descent is too far even for someone with a long history of no-ball-left-behind obsession (who has, nevertheless, left thousands of balls behind).

The tools at my disposal are an auspiciously-placed sapling for dangling from and the two-foot ballflinger gadget for reach-extending. Clutching both is the precariously outstretched body of a world-class dumbass.

"You know what's fun?" she asks. "If you fall and don't die, then you get to lay there in a broken heap and wonder which comes first, medevac or hungry locals."

"Oh hey, that *is* fun," I grumble as the sapling supporting my two hundred pounds grumbles too.

"Is that how you see me? Large-breasted? Big butt?"

"Now? Seriously?" I am still miles from the ball with no way to close the gap.

"Kind of sexual, don't you think? Would you like me to dance for you?"

"Don't make this weirder than it already is. It's not even me who said it, it was the old lady."

"You *are* the old lady," she says, annoyingly but not wrongly.

"I'm you, too," I say.

"That's way more than you know," she replies.

I have hung myself out too far. I've crossed the point of no return, no way up but down. The question of rescue versus getting eaten is not really valid because there's no hope of rescue.

"Is this to be your final chapter then? Death by folly?"

"Good as any and fitting for someone in my line. Maybe I was talking about some other goddess."

"There's only one."

"What does an old washerwoman on the Chinese border thousands of years ago know about goddesses?" I ask.

"What do *you* know about *her?*"

The sapling is about to give up on me. I have a plan, but it begins with transferring the long plastic ballflinger from my right hand to my tree hand.

"Maybe she's seen a statue in a roadside shrine or outside a rich man's house or in a temple."

"Why not just drop the ball-thrower thing like a normal person?"

"I didn't get where I am today by being a normal person."

"And where are you today? Suspended over a precipitous rockfall by a tree that was a seedling last year."

"I think of myself as a tree sometimes, an apple tree."

"The resemblance is uncanny. You have seconds to live, by the way."

"I'll survive the fall," I reply bravely.

"But not the night," she replies correctly.

"An apple tree, right? I do what I do, I produce a fruit. By their fruits shall ye know them. By my fruit I am known. The value of the tree is the fruit it produces. The fruit is the product, the tree is just the means of production. I produce fruit."

"Your books, I suppose."

"I make a mean BLT, but mainly the books, yes."

"I could go for a BLT right about now," she says.

"You have no other mouth but mine," I say. "An apple tree produces delicious and nutritious fruit but doesn't force anyone to eat it. The tree is not concerned with what becomes of the fruit, only production and release. Apples contain arsenic, which can be a poison or a purifier. Maybe a few apples get eaten, or maybe they all fall to the ground and rot. Maybe some seeds give rise to new trees, maybe not. It doesn't matter to the tree. The apple tree creates fruit, but does not reflect on the fruit of the fruit."

"You're making it up as you go."

"It's a work in progress."

"Can you even hold on like that?"

"Not sure. My hand is numb."

Trust the arch was my mantra in skydiving, especially in my first dozen jumps. It can sometimes happen when goofing around in freefall that you lose control and start tumbling, or just become disoriented, and that's when those words spring handily to mind; trust the arch. The arch is the attitude of safe canopy deployment; chest forward, facing into the fall, stable, in control despite being totally out of control. As soon as you think the words *trust the arch*, your body adopts them and you find yourself falling face down, arms and legs out, center of mass leading the way, now able to safely release your chute without getting tangled in the emerging cords.

I stick the ballflinger between my teeth and, in a single motion, release the sapling behind me with my left hand and catch a three-inch maple ahead of me with my right. I am now stretched out fifteen feet above a steep slope of jagged boulders and one tennis ball. My victory has a hollow feel.

"So you think an old washerwoman in ancient China would picture a goddess as having large breasts and a big butt?"

"Shapely behind," I say around the ballflinger in my mouth. "Yes, that's what came to mind."

"*Your* mind. That's how you see me?"

"You have many faces," I remind her.

The maple caught me but bent under my weight so my arch is now appropriate for skydiving but not for cliffhanging. I meant to arch upward but the tree bent too much and I'm bowed seriously downward. This position has no future.

"I'm pretty sure you're not a Taoist goddess."

"I am all gods and goddesses."

"Technically, sure, but I never really made the connection to you until you brought it up. No offense, but I think of you as an element of my own dreamstate."

"Like a book or a BLT."

"Or any other appearance."

"Including yourself and your current predicament."

"Yeah, I guess."

My left foot is wedged against a rock, my right hand is clutching the little maple, and the rest of me is straining against a strong downward tendency. I have often poked fun at the theory of gravity, but now it seems that gravity may have the last laugh. The maple is just a few feet down on a long, steep, rocky slope and the next stop is a long way further down. I have one final maneuver to try. Once I begin, gravity will take over and things will very quickly go either badly or terribly.

"Seconds from disaster."

"No shit."

I spit out the ballflinger and push off kind of sideways with my left foot so I can spring off a nearby root with my right which I accomplish with so-so success. That was the beauty part. The less beauty part is where I get my arms and legs clumsily wrapped around the maple and ride it down to earth. I don't manage to slow myself much, but I do manage not to go tumbling another fifty feet down the jagged slope. It's not pretty but it works. I still have problems, but being eaten isn't one of them.

"That had to hurt."

"Not dead."

Long pants mostly saved my tree-clenching thighs but my hands and forearms and part of my torso are a bit shredded. My right shoulder is jammed up and an unstuck landing did something to my left ankle. Still, not bad. I thank the maple tree and get shakily to my feet.

"Ouch," one of us says.

I look up and see Maya, the dog, on the path above staring down at me expectantly. She wants the ball. I clamber partway up the boulders, find the ballflinger in a tangle of brush and use it to reach between rocks and grab the tennis ball. I raise it high in unsung triumph. I toss the ball up to the trail and Maya runs after it. I toss the flinger up too, then lower myself back to my landing zone and fashion a walking stick. There's still a lot of downward potential to be resisted. Going slowly along and around and up, it takes me ten minutes to get back to where a simple walk went awry. I am not at the end of today's adventure; ankle, shoulder, and abrasions are becoming an issue and we're several miles from home with an hour until dark.

"So that's how you see me?"

"I don't know. What's the point of quibbling?"

"It passes the time," she says.

"Would you like to hear more about why I think of myself as an apple tree?"

"No."

We begin the long walk home. Maya, dog, ball in mouth, at my side.

"Does an apple tree wish it was in a different place producing different fruit? Does it aspire to swim or fly? My guess is that the apple tree is probably pretty busy being an apple tree and making apples. That's what it is, that's what it does. Same with me, right? Hello? Still there? I know you can hear me. Jesus, what's the point of an invis…"

I look down. Maya has dropped the ball. We turn back for it. Darkness falls.

Over the Moon

Not everything that counts can be counted,
and not everything that can be counted counts.

Albert Einstein

I FIGURED OUT PRETTY EARLY in life that grown-ups talk a lot of shit. I date this see-through vision back to when I tended bar at country club events and private parties at a much younger age than I could have done so in public establishments – which I never did – and during which time I was granted a painfully candid view of high-society grown-ups uninhibited, but it goes back before that. In the sixth grade, when I was eleven, I sat in class and listened to Mr. Larsen explain about the moon and tides and all that. I got kicked out of class that day for asking too many questions, or maybe for asking them in too snarky a tone.

By that age, I'd already ruined Santa Claus for a lot of kids a few years before they would have cracked it on their own. Santa is a sweet lie and nothing to condemn, but what was with this moon shit? I grew up on the Atlantic Ocean and the Long Island Sound and tides played an important part in my life, so when Mr. Larsen started talking about the moon creating the tides, it was the first time I really woke up in science class. My positive enthusiasm, however, was short-lived.

If lunar gravity can raise oceans, I pondered, what else can it lift? Do I weigh less when the moon is above? Can I jump higher or hit a baseball further? Let's go outside when the moon is up, I suggested in the first blush of scientific curiosity, and do some tests. If the moon's gravity can lift oceans, it will definitely pull up lighter stuff, right? Obviously, when the moon is above, regardless of phase, it's earth-gravity-defying gravity will make all the light stuff like hair and dust float upward, right?

The coolest thing to me was flying insects. When the moon was above, bugs above a certain weight would still have to work to stay aloft, and bugs right *at* that certain weight would be neutral and just float, but bugs below a certain weight would have to fly upside-down to resist the moonward pull, right? In fact, wouldn't all the floating particulate in our atmosphere have to follow the moon like a vertical compass needle? Up, west, down, east, up, west, down, east? I actually thought so at first. I was just extrapolating from the teacher's claims about lunar gravity; it wasn't until I started talking about insects flying upside-down that I heard how stupid it sounded.

Using his fancy pull-down moon chart, Mr. Larsen went on to explain that the earth actually deforms and elongates along the line between the centers of the earth and moon. That made me laugh. What shape is the non-spinning moon if it experiences the constant 6x pull of the earth? It looks round to us, but from the side, it must look like an egg or a pear. And between their combined gravity, why doesn't the moon get closer every minute and smash into us? If gravity is always changing, then you never know what anything weighs. It's like sitting on a scale on a roller coaster; sometimes you weigh double, sometimes half. I asked a bunch of questions that Mr. Larsen didn't seem to like. Maybe they were stupid questions and easily answered, but the point is that he didn't answer, he got huffy. He did a little tapdance thing where he explained that lunar gravity was a simplified explanation and that other factors like earth rotation and solar gravity played a part, but I clearly had him on his heels. You'd think that he, as an educator, would say something like, "Those are all good questions, laddie. I don't know the answers but I'll try to find out and get back to you tomorrow." But instead he said, "Go stand in the hall."

❖

I didn't figure out the Santa Claus thing on my own, and when I did, it wasn't because I had such an incisive, probing mind. Actually, our housekeeper Penny had her daughter over to help with the windows one day when I was seven, and she introduced me by saying, "Dis one still believe in Sanny Claus."

As soon as she said it, that belief snapped off like a switch in my head, like a mini *aha!* event. *Of course there's no goddamn Sanny Claus! A fat guy crawling down chimneys to leave presents for every kid in the world in one night? Magic elves? Flying reindeer? What the hell was I thinking?*

Now, in sixth-grade science class, something else was snapping off like a switch, and it wasn't just the moon, it was the myth of the all-knowing, truth-telling grown-up. This Larsen guy was talking out his ass. I, a little knucklehead, knew it, and he, a grown-up educator, didn't. He really believed what he was saying because, as a state-sanctioned indoctrinator, he was himself fully indoctrinated. He had been flipped into cud-munching, off-gassing, bovine mode years before and now his job was to flip us.

But more importantly, just as Sanny Claus had shown me something about adult deception, and just as private-event bartending would later provide me with insight into the hidden side of adults, so did lunar gravity show me something about schools and teachers and science. These people would say any crazy-ass shit as long as everyone went along with it, and they were trying to get us to fall into line with them. That's what was going on. Nowadays, I now have a clear-eyed view of the mass-sterilization process we call the education system, and even admire it for meeting society's need to incarcerate, indoctrinate and institutionalize its youth, but back then I was very conflicted about the whole thing. When I *don't* think, I discovered, everything seems one way, but when I *do* think, everything seems a totally different way, and all forces seem to be pushing me down the road of non-thinking. Even though I was never fully indoctrinated, it would still be a few more decades before I found my way back to where those two roads diverged and took the one less traveled.

❖

I sometimes wonder how things might be different if all those countless thousands of hours of life we flush away in school were put to some worthwhile use like actual exploration and discovery and growth instead of having our lovely little brains scooped out and replaced with steaming piles of dogshit. In a society of Adults, children would be guided into their own Adulthood, but in a society of Children, the young are neutered, lobotomized, and prepared for a life as herdmembers, bearing no resemblance to their potential.

The very idea of putting our formative years to good and happy use is so radical as to be practically unthinkable. What if young people were encouraged to explore and learn and develop instead of being herded and molded and homogenized? Such a revolutionary act would undermine the daycare component of the school mission because a true education – reading, writing, and reckoning – would require only a tiny fraction of the time we spend in classrooms having our curiosity smothered and our spirits broken. Young people might put that time to use for real learning instead of being tucked out of sight like larval hatchlings squirming in darkness.

But really, who cares about any of that? You can't change what was done to you and you probably can't do much for your own kids. The only thing you might be able to do is find your way back to where those two roads diverged and go the other way.

❖

A true and perfect philosophy of being, stripped of all belief and nonsense, is so simple and obvious as to hardly need stating. Here it is in forty-two words:

> Only two things exist, one of which doesn't. There is only awareness and appearance. Awareness is true and does exist. Appearance is untrue and does not exist. Awareness is the combination of infinite consciousness and perfect intelligence – Brahman – and that thou art.

And here it is in one:

> Dreamstate.

The dreamstate is reality. There is no other, better, *realer* reality out there waiting for us to discover it, there are only the broader dimensions of this reality into which we can expand and explore to the degree that we're able to shed the fear-based constraints of the false self and break loose of herd gravity. The problem is that understanding the dreamstate is both heretical *within* it and antithetical *to* it. We are restricted to a condition of perpetual childhood for good reason. Within the context of the dreamstate, our eyes are *supposed* to be closed. We are *supposed* to be emotionally governed and mentally impaired. The mass of men are *supposed* to live lives of quiet desperation. That's how the dramatic production of humanity works. We exist to amuse, it's all just drama for the sake of drama so nothing is really wrong and nothing needs to be fixed. Everything is just as it should be, including our belief that it's not.

Change begins by finding a loose thread and tugging on it. If God loves us, why is there evil and suffering? Are we predestined or do we possess free will? Why is the sky blue? Why don't little bugs fly upside-down under the moon? Every question has an answer and you already know how to find it, but it's up to you to do the work.

That might be a good thing to teach children; not how smart and advanced we are, but how domesticated, how emotionally enslaved and intellectually disabled, how vulnerable to fallacies and biases, how primitive and superstitious in belief, how cowardly in science and corrupt in academia, how bereft of knowledge and devoid of comprehension, and how desperate to inflict our mediocrity on future generations. We should teach the young not that *every*thing is settled but *nothing* is. Not how far we've come but how we've yet to take our first true step, which has nothing to do with science or religion or spirituality, and everything to do with restoring our altered development.

By tugging on any loose thread of consensus reality we can begin unraveling the entire tapestry of delusion. Once you start pulling, things start coming apart. Your tapestry is your own personal narrative of reality overlaying the universal energetic structure beneath. We all have our own cosmetic narrative, but we all share the same energetic structure. When narrative is dismantled, pattern is revealed. Ego-clad children dwell at the level of personal narrative. Ego-free adults merge into the impersonal level of pattern. Personal narrative defines the Segregated State of Human Childhood, universal pattern defines the Integrated State of Human Adulthood, and Nothing Forever defines enlightenment. This is the ABCs of being, and this is what we would have learned as children had adults been in charge.

Goddess I:
The Tao That Can Be Told

The Tao of the Large-Breasted
Goddess with the Shapely Behind

Legend has it that late in life, Chinese sage Lao Tzu got on his water buffalo and rode westward out of China. At the border, he was stopped and asked to write down his teachings before leaving. What follows is the true account of the events surrounding the writing of *The Tao Te Ching*.

In an isolated guardshack on China's mountainous western border, two soldiers in their mid-thirties, YIN and YANG, sit face to face playing a very focused game of Pinky Touch, the rules of which are unclear. Neither man moves, both silently intent on their almost-touching little fingers. After thirty seconds, the frozen tableau bursts into activity as Yin leaps up in victory and Yang collapses in defeat.

YIN

I am the Lord-Emperor of Pinky-Touch!

YANG

Yeah, yeah. You win again, your imperial highness. I gotta take a leak.

YIN

On the other side of the pissing rock this time, please.

YANG

Yeah, yeah.
returning a few moments later
Well, you don't see that every day.

YIN

See what?

YANG

An old man coming up through the pass riding a water buffalo.

YIN

An old man coming up through the pass riding a water buffalo heading *out* of China? No one has passed this way in fourteen years, and now we have an *old man* coming up through the pass riding a *water buffalo* heading *out* of China? This calls for paperwork!

YANG

Do we have any paper left? I thought we used it all for...

YIN

They sent us fresh papers with the last resupply five years ago. I've been hiding it.

Yin and Yang are busy tidying up for company when there's a knock on the door. Yang rushes to answer, Yin holds him back.

YIN

quietly to Yang

Let's try to savor this.

YANG

quietly to Yin

Good idea! It could be fourteen years before we have another guest.

YIN

aloud, sing-song

Who's the-ere?

STRANGER

Just an old man and his Bubby seeking shelter for the night.

YANG

One minute, please. You caught us right in the middle of, uh, brushing our teeth.

They open the door to find LAO TZU *standing outside holding the reins of a water buffalo.*

LAO TZU

Oh wow, you guys are soldiers? Well, me and my Bubby were just passing through, and I thought we should stop in and say, you know, hi. Hi.

YIN

Hi. Actually, we're border guards. You're about to leave China.

LAO TZU

No shit?

YANG

No shit.

YIN

And there's actually some paperwork involved.

LAO TZU

No shit?

YANG

No shit. Not an everyday occurrence, an old man on a water buffalo leaving China.

YIN

Still, no bother, glad to have you. We'll sort you out and have you on your way in no time.

LAO TZU

Well, alright. Where can I park my...?

YIN

Ah, your Bubby, yes. Imperial Border Guard Second Class Yang will take care of her for you. Please step inside and have a seat.

Yang goes out to take care of Bubby. Yin and Lao Tzu sit across from each other at a table. Yin lays out his forms.

YIN

Alrighty then, let's get started. Name?

LAO TZU

Venerable Master.

YIN

Say what?

LAO TZU

Venerable Master.

YIN

Okay, we'll come back to that. Occupation?

LAO TZU

Occupation?

YIN

Yes, what do you do?

LAO TZU

Well, that's a little tricky, I don't actually *do* anything. I'm more of a Wu Wei kind of guy.

Yang returns from tending to Bubby.

YANG

What's Wu Wei?

LAO TZU

Oh, you know, uh, non-exertion, basically. The spiritual art of not-doing. It's harder than it sounds.

YANG

It would have to be.

YIN

I have a long list of jobs here, friend, we just have to check a box. Pig wrangler? Noodle bender? Tea-leaf reader?

LAO TZU

I'm just kind of, you know, a person.

YIN

checking list

Person, person... Sorry, not on the list. Help me out here, I have to put something down. Barefoot doctor? Silkworm farmer? Foot binder? Poet?

LAO TZU

Oh, well, poet maybe. That sounds nice.

YANG

You're a poet?

LAO TZU

Yes.

YANG

Do you write poems?

LAO TZU

No, not really.

YANG

Then you're not a bloody poet, are ya?

YIN

Well then, I can't put that on the form. What is it that you actually *do* do?

LAO TZU

It's not really something I do, it's more like what I *am*. I'm kind of like a philosopher-at-large, a wandering sage.

YANG

I doubt that'll be on the list.

YIN

Yep, here it is! Sage comma wandering.

LAO TZU

Really?

YIN

Yeah, just after sadhu comma itinerant and right before saint comma roaming.

LAO TZU

Oh, I see. You're having fun with me.

YANG

How about warrior? I bet that's on the list.

LAO TZU

Sure, warrior is good, like poet-warrior maybe.

YIN

It's more than my life is worth to say an old man with no poems is a poet and no weapon is a warrior. And anyway, it's not on the list.

LAO TZU

How about Wise Man?

YANG

Wise Man?

LAO TZU

Yeah, like someone who goes around spreading wisdom.

YIN

checking

Wise man, wise man... Uh yeah, that one actually *is* on the list. "Wise Man: Someone who goes around spreading wisdom." Wow. Is that really a thing?

LAO TZU

Well, there's no union or guild, but I guess it's a thing. It's on the list, right?

YIN

Yep, it's on the list.

YANG

Any money in the Wise Man game?

LAO TZU

Uh, no, not really. It's not like that.

YANG

Girls? Groupies? Hotshot friends? Get invited to all the best parties?

LAO TZU

Not so much.

YANG

Then it's just kind of, what, exactly?

LAO TZU

Just kind of its own thing, I guess.

YANG

Yeah? That's cool. Whaddaya go by? Wise man? Professor?

LAO TZU

Master is fine.

YANG

Nothing too hoity-toity. That's nice.

YIN

Well, your name is Venerable Master. I guess that should have tipped us off.

YANG

Wow, your parents were really shooting for the stars.

LAO TZU

Yeah, funny how that worked out.

YIN

Okay, okay, we're doing great, almost done. In your role as a, uh, wise man, what is it that you actually do?

LAO TZU

Do? Well, um, nothing really, you know, just be wise and stuff.

YIN

writing

Just be wise and stuff, got it. So you have an occupation in which you get paid nothing for doing nothing except being wise?

YANG

And stuff.

YIN

Yes, and stuff. Moving on. Next of kin?

LAO TZU

Why? What for?

YANG

Oh, you know, in case some corrupt border guards decide to throw you off a cliff and eat your Bubby, who do we call?

LAO TZU

Call?

YIN

Contact. Your people. Who are your people?

LAO TZU

I don't have any people. I'm kind of a solo deal. So, is that it? Am I free to go?

YIN

What's the rush, friend?

YANG

Yeah, you don't do anything, you don't get paid anything, you don't have any people. I guess you can be a Wise Man pretty much anywhere, right?

LAO TZU

Well, it's not quite that...

YIN

Uh oh! We have an asterisk!

YANG

Oh dear.

LAO TZU

An asterisk? What's that?

YIN

It's a small star-shaped chara...

LAO TZU

Yes, I know what it *is*, but what does it *mean?*

YIN

It means before we let you leave China, we have to ask if you have anything to declare.

LAO TZU

Declare? No, not really. Just me and my Bubby.

YANG

You got a receipt for your Bubby?

YIN

I was thinking more about your wisdom.

LAO TZU

My what?

YIN

Your wisdom. You're a wise man, right?

LAO TZU

Well, yeah, I mean, for the paperwork...

YANG

Oh yeah, that's right! If you're a wise man you gotta have some wisdom. Only makes sense.

LAO TZU

Uh okay, maybe. I mean, I guess I have some wisdom.

YIN

Great, let's have it.

YANG

Yeah, spit it out, Maestro.

LAO TZU

Spit what out?

YIN

The wisdom. You can't take it out of the country. You'll have to leave it with us.

LAO TZU

Are you having fun with me again?

YIN

No, we're not having fun with you.

YANG

Do we look like we're having fun with you?

LAO TZU

I don't know. When was the last time anyone came through here?

YANG

Yesterday.

YIN

Never.

YANG

Oh yeah, never.

YIN

We've been here for fourteen years and you're the first, but I'm afraid the rules are very clear on this point.

YANG

Yeah, you said it yourself, wisdom is like poetry.

LAO TZU

I don't think I said that.

YANG

If you were a poet, we'd have to make sure you left your poems behind.

YIN

So you don't deprive your homeland of the fruit of your labors during your time with us, but instead of poems, you have wisdom.

YANG

Yeah, so fork it over.

LAO TZU

Um, I don't... I mean, uh, I can't...

YIN

Can't?

YANG

Oh dear.

LAO TZU

Well, it doesn't really work that way. I don't have a pocketful of wisdom I can just pull out and hand over.

YIN

Oh, I'm sorry to hear that.

YANG

Yeah, I was looking forward to some good wisdom.

LAO TZU

Sorry to disappoint. Am I free to go now?

YIN

Sure, yes, absolutely. Back into China, though. I'm afraid we can't let you leave with your wisdom.

YANG

And we'll have to impound your water buffalo pending some clarification on license, title, taxes, and insurance.

LAO TZU

So I can go back into China without my Bubby, but we can't leave the country?

YANG

Right.

YIN

Or you can stay here. We can set up a nice bed of straw for you.

YANG

And a nice bed of rice for Bubby.

LAO TZU

What? No, you can't eat my Bubby!

YANG

We're just laying out your options.

YIN

Yeah, it's just this darned career choice you made.

YANG

Our bosses are sticklers about asset leakage.

YIN

Including wisdom.

YANG

Especially wisdom, I should think.

YIN

It's considered a national treasure. I'm sure you understand.

LAO TZU

Well, I mean, a might be able to jot down a few lines…

YIN

Oh, could you?

YANG

That would be lovely.

YIN

We can't leave big blanks areas on the form. Gets us in hot water with the higher-ups.

YANG

Literally.

YIN

Testy bunch, the higher-ups. Given to extremes in the old punishment department.

YANG

Always trying to outdo each other. You don't
want to know.

YIN

But if you were to give us some wisdom we
could use to complete the form...

YANG

Well, that's really all we need.

YIN

Right, a complete form.

*Yin turns the parchment over and prepares to
write.*

Okay, please begin.

LAO TZU

Well, okay, I guess I don't have a choice. Let's see,
okay. Ready? Okay, here we go.

clears throat

The Tao...

YIN

Stop!

YANG

The *what?*

I Call It Consciousness

> There was something undifferentiated and yet
>   complete, which existed before Heaven and
>   Earth.
> Soundless and formless, it depends on nothing
>   and does not change.
> It operates everywhere and is free from danger.
> It may be considered the mother of the universe.
> I do not know its name; I call it Tao.
>
> *Tao Te Ching, ch. 25*

I N SPIRITUALITY, THERE ARE ONLY THREE possible objectives: The Grand Prize, which is
Human Adulthood; the Consolation Prize, which
is Contentment in Captivity; and the Booby Prize,
which is Spiritual Enlightenment. Some might argue
for a fourth category, Adventures in Consciousness,
achieved via meditation, breathwork, entheogens, neo-
shamanism and so on, but those are just broader and
less traveled dimensions of the dreamstate and only
qualify for the consolation prize.

⬦

Just as the only point of Zen is awakening *from* the dreamstate, the only point of Taoism is awakening *within* it; enlightenment and adulthood respectively. Neither Zen nor Taoism is a flock-and-shepherd deal or a guru-chela deal because they're both about hard transition, not soft growth. They're both binary; black and white, no shades of gray. In theory they're both built for transition, but in practice they're both used for growth. I've been asked if I endorse Taoism as a path to adulthood or Zen as a path to enlightenment, and the answer in both cases is no. There are two reasons for this; one, they've both been co-opted and corrupted into mere parodies of their potential, and two, you're better off without them. Where you are now is Point A and the black hole within is Point B, so how much teaching, tradition and technique do you really need? If your heart and mind are focused you'll succeed, and if they're not, it doesn't matter what costume you wear or game you play. Open your eyes and all will be revealed. Nothing is hidden or withheld and your chains have no locks, so the only one holding you back is you.

⬦

I, like you perhaps, live in my own private universe. I call it by names like reality and dreamstate, but it's never more than the sum total of what appears to my awareness. My dreamstate universe at any moment consists of whatever I'm aware of in that moment. Right now the moon doesn't exist for me... well, okay, *now* it does because I just started thinking about it, but just before that it didn't and in another moment it won't again. It's the same with all the senses, emotions, memories and thoughts that I'm not presently sensing, feeling, remembering or thinking. I am awareness, and what I am aware *of* at any given moment is my reality *in* that moment.

Your reality and your awareness are the same thing. A tree falling in a forest makes a sound if you hear it and doesn't if you don't. If you watch a tree fall on a muted TV, did it make a sound? You can argue yes, but the obvious truth is no; you are the sole arbiter of your dreamstate reality, and you heard no sound. Perception doesn't *create* reality, it *is* reality; the only one you have. You may believe there are others, but you can only know our own. That's not some crazy-ass belief, it's just a simple observation. Most people would say that the tree *does* make a sound because there's obviously a universe independent of their awareness, but it's not obvious, it's an assumption, and well worth revisiting. Awareness picks up bits and pieces of appearance and mind fills in the rest, but what if there is no rest?

By controlling appearance – what you think, sense, feel, and believe – you control your reality. You decide if it's a mountain forest or a city sewer. My reality is sensitive to my thoughts, and my thoughts are responsive to my environment; not that I'm easily influenced, but that I like to keep my inner space free of toxic, distorting and polluting influences, which are generated invariably and exclusively by juvenile humans. The dramatic human theater is a nice place to visit, but I don't want to live there. Observing human drama doesn't affect me much, but being exposed to the thoughts, feelings, opinions, and beliefs of human children does. As if by harmonic entrainment, my inner space starts adapting and responding to those around me and turns into a pigsty. For this reason, I can't listen to talk radio, I never linger within earshot of private conversations, and the last TV commercial I saw was five years ago. That's what the sewer metaphor represents; that chaotic, discordant, demon-infested environment that infects you and drags you down. It doesn't matter how it got into you, all that matters is getting it out. Then, once out of the sewer and back in the sun, it's like it never happened.

That's why I'm uncomfortable in an ego-dense environment; why I have gravitated away from the things of man and why I assume any adult would feel compelled to do the same. I'm still entertained by humanity, but now I access it mostly through screens which I can control and turn off when I've had enough. By their fruits shall ye know them, and the sole fruit of humanity is amusing tragicomic spectacle. It's like nature is my bedroom and mankind is my entertainment room, so I have the best of both worlds; I reside in nature and watch human spectacle like a movie.

My dreamstate reality seems to work in a consistent, predictable, clockwork-like manner. It appears that I exist in time and space, in a body and environment of energy and matter, but I know that none of that is true because I know beyond any possibility of error that only consciousness exists. I didn't arrive at this conclusion through scientific calculation, religious belief, or by subscribing to an all-inclusive philosophy. I arrived at it through a personal journey of untruth unrealization. It's not what I believe, but what remains when belief is gone. Once you complete this brick-by-brick dismantling of Maya's palace, the remaining truth is so simple and obvious that it's hard to believe you didn't see it the whole time. As long as emotion governs intellect, life can only be a blur, but when you switch control from heart to mind, everything resolves into perfect clarity.

Appearance doesn't exist, but it does *appear* to exist. That's weird, but that's how dreams are. The key that unlocks the mystery is that I am not the dreamer because there is no I. I am, at most, the distorting influence of the light that passes through me, like film distorts the light of the projector to create anything from a cinematic masterpiece to incoherent static. The term I Am/Consciousness does not refer to myself as a discrete unit of selfhood, but as a timeless, spaceless point of awareness. That's where asking *Who am I?* will get you; not to true self but to no-self. That's where the line is drawn. That line is represented by the circle of the yinyang symbol which divides the true paradigm of infinite unity from the false paradigm of finite duality. All the black in the yinyang symbol, including the circle, represents finite appearance. Remove the black and what remains is the infinite white field of featureless awareness, and that thou art.

◈

There are two Taos, the one that can't be spoken and the one that can. The one that can't be spoken is what I call consciousness and the one that can is what I call pattern. The Tao that *can* be spoken is the operating system of the human adult − flow energy effortless doing, right-action, etc − and the Tao that *can't* be spoken is the truth of you; featureless awareness. The realization of the former is adulthood and the realization of the latter is enlightenment. The reason we can't speak of the Tao that can't be spoken is that it's featureless and infinite and otherless, so we call it the mother of all things and leave it at that. Of the Tao that *can* be spoken we can speak all day; smooth effortless functioning, non-doing, Wu Wei, right-action, right-knowing, manifestation, flow, pattern, integration, subtle energy dynamics, and so on. That's the adulthood you'd be enjoying right now if you hadn't been assimilated by the collective.

Transitioning to adulthood is success and everything else is irrelevant. Who cares if you have ten gold medals or ten great kids or ten billion dollars if you're a ten-year-old kid in a grown-up's body? Who cares if you're the best Borg in the collective if you're still a Borg in the collective? Nothing comes before your own transition to adulthood, but that can never happen until you realize that a), there is such a thing, and b), you could be there, but c), you're not.

As with anyone caught in Maya's silvery web, aspiring Taoists would disagree with me because they don't know they're trapped in the halfborn state. The difference between Child and Adult is as clear in spirit as it is in body, but if you believe yourself fully and normally developed, then what hope is there that you'll seek out and subject yourself to the rigors of a death-rebirth transition? If you're content as a caterpillar among caterpillars who know nothing of butterflies, then your journey is over before it ever began.

It's not Taoism's fault that it has been flipped to its own negative pole; it happens to all good things. If I were to create my own system – Aletheology or Jedvaita, for instance – it would quickly devolve to its own negative aspect. Instead of awakening the spiritual anarchist within, it would be absorbed by ego and converted into a child-safe version in which maxims like No Belief Is True and No-Self Is True Self go on t-shirts and tattoos, where everyone has a Border Collie and skydiving is a spiritual practice. *"Follow the shoe!" "No! Follow the gourd!"* And who would awaken? No one, not ever, because the dreamstate is ruled by

Maya and your reality is her domain. She controls us from within as ego – the intelligence of fear – so if we want to be free of her, we have to root her out like a system-wide infection, even though it kills the host.

◈

Wu Wei might best be described as the spiritual sense of balance. It is not a mystical power, it's just the way things work when we open our eyes, lower our shields, and relax into the natural flow of being. That's the watercourse way, but ego has us swimming against the current. Wu Wei comes standard with Adulthood, but it's always available to everyone to whatever degree we allow it. Anyone can avail themselves of it because it's the structural underlayment of personal reality. It's always there, just below the surface. You don't have to go out and acquire it because it's already yours; you just have to stop pushing it away. Manifestation, intuition, insight, smooth functioning and effortless doing, right-action, right-knowing, and being in the flow are all the natural result of operating at the global level of energetic pattern instead of the local level of personal narrative. We all have experiences of effortless functioning at times because that universal substructure is always there, just beneath the surface, whether we reside at that level or we just popped in for a visit. There's no effort involved, just a release into the prevailing energetic currents which, if we can peel our deathgrip off the tiller for a moment, will do all the work and make all the decisions and guide us effortlessly and unerringly into alignment. Then, when fear and distrust regain control, ego-pilot is reengaged and a state of functioning misalignment is restored.

Well-developed Adults can get snapped out of alignment, but they snap back pretty easily. I won't ask you to look up Valentine Michael Smith, but that was a living Taoist Master if ever there was one. Sonaya is the oldest person I know in this sense, and she never seems to get yanked out of alignment. I myself am mostly in, but I find it amusing to get pulled out now and then. Anger, tiredness and confusion can disrupt me, but usually only for a moment and then I chuckle at myself for being such a dope and settle back into place. This is especially annoying when someone cuts me off in traffic and I want to enjoy a healthy expression of road rage, but the anger impulse erupts as laughter.

My unshakable assumption is that all Human Children, were they able to make an informed choice, would sell the house, sell the car, sell the kids, and make a make-or-break, do-or-die dash towards Adulthood. That seems unthinkable from one perspective and a no-brainer from another. Since virtually everyone everywhere is unknowingly stuck in the halfborn state, I naturally look at everyone as being wrong about everything all the time. Taoists might be reckoned the least wrong because Taoism is shaped by the real and accessible prospect of adulthood.

However, the child side of the equation – getting to adulthood – and the adult side of the equation – living as an adult – are two separate and unrelated fields. *Getting* there is about transition and *being* there is about growth. Growth is a normal process of both childhood and adulthood, but it doesn't link them, and because the transition is a paradigm-shift, even the youngest Adult is a different order of being than even the oldest Child.

Using myself as a handy example of life in the Integrated State, I don't make any conscious effort to function effortlessly. It's not that I don't think about things or make decisions, it's more like I'm patient; I wait for the way forward to make itself known, and then I step into that future. It's not that I don't do anything, but that I don't act until the way forward appears, and then it's not so much a doing as an unfolding. I never seem to do anything I don't want to do, yet I leave nothing undone. It's like driving cross-country; one radio station comes into range and you listen to that while it's clear, then it fades and another one comes in for a while before it fades, and so on. You can't do anything to make a weak signal come in better, you can either take it as it comes or learn to put up with a lot of static. If you insist on receiving news at noon and classic rock at two and talk radio at four, you're going to misalign yourself with the reality of

your situation and make things unpleasant for yourself, but if you relax and enjoy whatever's coming in
clearly, you'll have a much nicer time of it.

I observe pattern and move with it, not by trying
but by allowing. I don't command my environment or
bend the universe to my will; my will and the universal will are the same will. I reside in a state of effortless
functioning so naturally that I'm unaware of it until
I slip out of it. This has been my standard mode of
operation for decades, not because I read it in a book
or because some jammy-clad master of serenity beat it
into me, but because I underwent an initial transition
and a fair amount of subsequent growth. Wu Wei is
not the sole domain of mystic masters, it's the normal
cocreative relationship between any human and their
dreamstate reality.

❖

Using you as a handy example of life in the
Segregated State, you are confined to your state by
fear-based emotional attachments; the need to project
and maintain your self-image foremost among them.
Maybe you think all this adulthood stuff sounds
pretty cool, but you have the job and the kids and
the house and bills and friends and family. Great, but
keep in mind that you don't really have all that, all
that has you. Keep in mind that those attachments
form the very steel and cement of your cell. Keep in
mind also that anyone who tells you that you can keep

your attachments *and* expand into adulthood – that it's a matter of growth and not transition, that you can have a rebirth without first a death – is telling you exactly what you want to hear, and that's why you're drawn to them. The merchants and vendors in the spiritual marketplace will tell you that whatever path you choose can be tailored to fit your existing lifestyle. That's the lie that you insist on being told, the used car you insist on being sold. It's not a flaw in spiritual systems; their real but unstated purpose is to steer you toward the consolation prize of content-ment in containment. They promise that you can get there from here, but the real spiritual path calls for the destruction of the false – self included – and that's something no one is in the market for.

It may be tolerant and compassionate and inclusive to embrace all spiritual teachings, but it won't get you one step closer to your goal. When playtime is over, there are not a thousand spiritual paths, or hundreds or dozens or even two, there's only one; to and through the black hole within. Your head is stuck in a trap and you can do one of two things; make yourself comfort-able or chew your way out. There are a million ways to make yourself comfortable, but the only way to chew your way out is one bite at a time.

If you want to transition to adulthood, my advice would be to steer clear of Taoism. Nice people, I'm sure, but as with any subsection of the great herd, they have this whole thing turned around. Like so many others, they think the way to become a butterfly is by acting like one. The idea that you become a rockstar by impersonating a rockstar is fine in the theatrical sense of playing a character, but not in the authentic sense of figuring out who and what and where you really are. This is a chronic misconception of halfborns and the defining deception of the spiritual marketplace.

Such highly revered systems of human spirituality as Buddhism, Taoism, and Hinduism are devised by ego and Maya for the purpose of keeping you in place, not making a journey. I hope the hows-and-whys of this are obvious to you by now. I hope that your eyes are open enough to see the subtle dynamics of fear and delusion that engineer our captivity, undermine our capacity for reason, and retard our propensity for growth. I hope that by now you can look at the spiritual marketplace from above instead of within and see it for the place where dreams go to die. But most of all, I hope you're having a nice adventure. It ends, you know.

Marichelle 7:
A Pretty Big Problem

> The big secret is no secret at all. It's just sitting
> there in case you want to look. I'm looking at it
> right now and I'm not even trying. Everywhere I
> look, there it is, so not a very big secret really.

Marichelle

MARICHELLE IS AWAKE. She is from Switzerland and now lives on an island off Honduras. In response to many requests, she gave a one-time series of talks in English to a small group. The transcript of these talks has been provided to me with permission to use. Attempts to organize this material only seem to make things worse, so I'm just presenting the best of it in loosely strung-together bite-sized bits. The talks were lively, but audience interactions have not been retained. I have made minor changes for readability.

Thinking and seeing are the same thing like believing and dreaming are the same thing. If you want to stay in coma you have to use believing. If you want to come out of coma you have to use thinking.

*

Believing and dreaming are very nice but they don't let you go anywhere. Thinking is not very nice but if you want to go anywhere you have to do it. You can't just make a wish. There's no magic wand you can just wave around.

*

There's nothing wrong about believing everything unless you want to stop doing it, then it's bad. The real thing is what you really want and what you say you want. It's good for those to be the same.

*

Everything is just what it is. If you don't like this kind of thing, don't even worry about it. Why make a thing if it's not a thing? Maybe you're still at that question. Maybe it's not even a thing for you.

*

You should know the difference between what's a thing and what's not a thing. Maybe you're saying it's a thing when it's not, but then why are you here, I wonder. Try asking that one for starters.

*

If you want to stay like you are there's no problem, but if you want to go forward there's a problem. Saying there's no problem is not a good plan. There's a pretty big problem.

*

There's a problem with your understanding so that's something you need to have some thought about. It's more of a problem if you don't know about it, so basically, try to know about it. This is where thinking can help.

*

There's no real stuff going on, just fake stuff to make everything seem interesting. Maybe you don't care about that but don't be quick to judge. Why should real be better than fake? It's a serious question.

*

There are many games to play, people play many games. You can play many games or just play one game. This is what I think is a good one, but it's really just whatever you like.

✳

Thinking is the key and we already have it, so why don't we use it? Thinking is the right tool for the job but we're too scared to use it. We have the key, so why we don't open the door is a good question.

✳

My job is what? I tell you there's a door and you have a key. That's my little job for what we're doing here. Then I go back to my life and you go back to yours. What you do with your life is up to you. I like to knit and play with my dogs. I think there's a cat around here too.

✳

I should teach you to knit, not this other business. With knitting you can actually make useful things. This other business probably does you no good but on a cold morning a warm shawl is a real thing.

✳

Nothing is what you think, or maybe everything is not what you think. Maybe both are right. Maybe they mean the same thing. The more you try the harder it gets, or maybe the farther you go the further it gets, something like that.

＊

The more you try to understand things the worse it gets. You don't make muddy water clear by swishing it around, you have to wait and let it settle down, right? You have to be relaxed about it which might be pretty hard. You want fast results so you keep swishing.

＊

We can break everything down to inside and outside. That's it, that's everything. Inside you can know, outside you never know. That's the difference. We think there's only one side. That's true, but it's not the side you think.

＊

It's usually fine and you just go along and have a nice time, but now you want to change or do something else maybe. Now you're talking to me and I can only talk about one thing. Coming out of coma and knitting. Okay, that's two things. And dogs. Three. And maybe the cat.

＊

Everything you think is real, all the way down to the most inside of yourself, is not real. That's all just coma stuff. Pretty crazy I know. You are a part of your coma just as much as the doorbell or your shoes or something.

✳

As far as you go inside, it's all coma. You have to keep going until you get past all that and there's nothing left. Then you're getting somewhere. That's where all the confusion suddenly makes sense.

✳

Emotion always wants to go back into coma but thinking always wants to go out. I never thought about this before but it seems like a good point even if I'm not saying it right. It's confusing because emotion is also a big part of coming out of coma and being out of coma, just not the biggest part.

✳

Don't worry about how smart you are, this isn't like that. This is about something different like how good you can think, which isn't the same as how smart. Even if you were the smartest person ever, this is true. You haven't even tried thinking yet so you don't know what it can do.

*

See how tricky it all is? But also pretty simple. Very tricky but pretty simple. No wonder no one gets this figured out. Pretty tricky, I would say, but also pretty simple.

*

Even the smartest person doesn't get close. They want to understand things as they seem, so they are not even in the right place to do good thinking. Being smart doesn't matter if you're looking in the wrong place. I would say that being smart is not a big advantage based on results.

*

Just logic is all you need, but then you have to go where logic tells you. That's not too easy which is why no one figures it out. No one even looks, but when you look, there it is.

*

It's a thing where you really have to do it, not just talk about it, or else it all seems like nonsense. I'm aware of that. Talking is easier than doing. This is something you can confirm in your own life.

*

I know you think you think but you really only feel you think. In normal life we are mostly all feeling and almost no thinking. If you change that even a little you can change a lot. Try it sometime, you'll see.

*

It's good to know what you can't know, like what nobody can know and what can't be known. You can't know what can't be known but you can know what you can't know. I don't think I'm saying this the best way but it's really true.

*

There's no manual for this like you get with your camera or your fishing pole. There are no people you can call for answers like a hotline. You have to find everything out for yourself or you never find it out.

*

It's all just playtime, no big deal. You come for a nice visit, play some nice games and then it's over. It's something to do. There are different games, that's all. I like this one. I didn't always like it so much but I like it now.

Goddess II:
Darkness within Darkness

YANG

What the hell is the *Tao?*

LAO TZU

Well, yeah, that's where we start running into some issues. You can't really *say* what it is. If you *can* say what it is, then that's definitely *not* what it is.

YIN

Oh dear, we're not getting off to a good start.

YANG

Is there gonna be a lot of talk about this Tao thing? If it's not a big deal maybe we can just skip past this part.

YIN

Yeah, good idea.

LAO TZU

No! The Tao is like the *main* thing. Everything hinges on this. All things hang from the Tao like pearls from a thread.

YIN

writes that down, reads it, scratches it out
So the Tao is like the main thing, but you can't say what it is?

LAO TZU

Right.

YANG

And if you *do* say what it is, you're wrong.

LAO TZU

Right.

YANG

The paper-pushers back at HQ are not gonna like this.

YIN

Yeah, they can be a little anal.

LAO TZU

The words of truth are always paradoxical.

YIN

I'll write that down, but it won't help.

YANG

What do we have so far, Yin?

YIN

Um, the uh, *Tao* is a thing where you can't say what it is, and if you *do* say what it is, you're wrong. And it's like a necklace, I guess.

YANG

Okay, that's a start. We can work with that. And how do we go about *seeing* this Tao of yours?

LAO TZU

Er, *you* can't actually see it.

YANG

Why not?

LAO TZU

Well, because you're not a sage. You're just, you know, regular.

YIN

But *you* can see it?

LAO TZU

Oh yeah, sure. All the time.

YANG

Like right now?

LAO TZU

Uh, yep.

YANG

Where? Point.

LAO TZU

Well, I mean, it's everywhere, isn't it? It's everything. There's nothing that's *not* it.

YIN

So why can't *we* see it?

YANG

Yeah, we see all the same stuff you see.

LAO TZU

Right, sure, good question. Well, you see, *you* see the surface of things. You see the superficial world. You see heaven and earth and the ten thousand things, but the Tao is like the thing behind all that.

YANG

Let me stop you there, Maestro. If we want to see this Tao thing of yours, we can't.

LAO TZU

Right. Well, you can see what it's *not*, but not what it *is*.

YANG

Sounds like a load of buffalo dung. You can see what the Tao *is*, but we can only see what it's *not?*

LAO TZU

I know how that sounds, but yeah. You see the manifestation, I see the source. Sorry.

YIN

No, that's okay. It's fine. That's the wisdom part, I suppose. If it made sense we'd all be wise and you'd be out of a job, right?

LAO TZU

Yeah, I guess.

YIN

The problem is, strictly in terms of the paperwork you see, I feel like we might be a little heavy on the paradox. The higher-ups aren't really known for their appreciation of irony and contradiction, even when it's in a wisdomy context. Perhaps you could take the sagely doubletalk down a notch and say something that actually makes sense?

LAO TZU

Um, sure, okay. Benefit comes from what is there. Usefulness from what is not there. How's that?

YIN

Uh, not great.

YANG

I say we throw the old man off the cliff and eat the water buffalo. Who's gonna know?

YIN

I think what my associate is trying to say is, would you please elaborate on that point?

LAO TZU

Uh, sure. Take this teacup for example. The cup provides us with a benefit of containment, but its usefulness is not because of what *is* there but what's *not* there.

YANG

He's totally messing with us.

LAO TZU

Or like that wall. The wall is the benefit, but the window is the usefulness. See? The wall is there, but the window is useful by being *not* there.

YANG

If we're attacked with flaming arrows you won't think so.

LAO TZU

Or like your minds. They're like teacups that are already full, so I can't really pour fresh knowledge into them, can I?

YIN

Blame-shifting is not a good way to go here.

LAO TZU

The cup is useful for what's not there. You can't drink tea from a lump of clay, right? Benefit comes from somethingness, but usefulness comes from nothingness. Well, you know, sometimes.

YANG

I'm picturing a fresh-dug grave.

LAO TZU

Exactly! It's useful because it's empty. If you fill it with... Oh, yes, I see.

YIN

Let's stick with the teacup for now, shall we?

LAO TZU

Yes, okay. We're talking about the potential state. An empty cup has unlimited potential, a full cup has no potential. Its usefulness is in its emptiness. A cup, a window, a grave, the hub of a wheel, it's their emptiness that makes them useful, right?

YIN

Okay, so?

YANG

Yeah, so?

LAO TZU

Well, you know, it's a work in progress. You can't just ask someone to start saying a lot of wise stuff right off the top of their head. It's a process. Observational wisdom, like, hey, you ever notice how a few minutes after you eat Chinese food, you're hungry again? Like, what's that all about, right?

YANG

I have *not* noticed that. And you don't have to say *Chinese* food, you can just say food.

YIN

Yes, Chinese is assumed. Okay, let's forget the teacup business. Try something else.

LAO TZU

The Tao begat one, one begat two, two begat three and three begat the ten thousand things.

YANG

Okay, now we're gettin' somewhere.

LAO TZU

The ten thousand things carry the positive and embrace the negative.

YIN

They do?

LAO TZU

Sure, the ten thousand things achieve harmony by combining positive and negative, see? You have to have both.

YIN

Okay. Please provide an example.

YANG

Yeah, like what?

LAO TZU

Well, like anything. Man-woman, high-low, inhale-exhale, light-dark, big-small. Everything has two sides, right? And even though they're not always equal, they're always in balance.

YIN

Er, maybe we could use an illustration, like a symbol or a pictogram or something.

LAO TZU

Okay, draw a picture of two fish swimming in a bowl, one white, one black, kind of chasing each other around in circles.

Yin draws the yinyang symbol.

YIN

Wow, what a great symbol! What do you call it?

LAO TZU

I call it the Lao Tzu symbol. It represents the dual nature of reality, you know, the harmony and balance of opposites.

YANG

The name could use some work.

YIN

And what does the bowl represent?

LAO TZU

The finite and dualistic nature of reality.

YIN

Meaning?

LAO TZU

Well, everything finite has a beginning, a middle
and an end, right? So heaven and earth and the
ten thousand things are all finite, meaning they
seem real but they're really not. The Tao, on the
other hand, has no beginning, middle or end. It
just goes on like, you know, forever.

YANG

And how do you know all this?

LAO TZU

Well, it stands to reason.

YANG

I'm not sure it does.

YIN

Okay, so there's the main thing, which is the
Tao, and there's all the other stuff, which is like
heaven and earth and the ten thousand things

and us, right?

LAO TZU

Right, but only the Tao is real. Everything else
is just, you know...

YIN

No, I don't know.

LAO TZU

Well, like, not real, right? Like impermanent,
fleeting. The ten thousand things represent all
the little comings and goings while the Tao
itself is like, you know, the *always* part.

YANG

We have a beginning, a middle and an end, so
that means we're not real? We don't exist?

LAO TZU

Correct. We're fleeting, like a passing thought or
a brief spark in the eternal night. First we're not,
then we are, then we're not again. Life is but a
dream, but the Tao abideth forever.

YANG

aside to Yin

Whaddaya think?

YIN

I don't know. It sounds okay coming out of
his mouth, but it looks totally bonkers on a
government form. We're soldiers, we're not in

the wisdom game.

YANG

Well, it sounds better than that Confucius guy. That guy gives me a headache.

YIN

Yeah, but *that* guy's not sitting in our shack, *this* guy is.

YANG

Well, let's keep going and see what happens. Worst case, we eat like kings tonight.

YIN

Emperors.

YANG

Oh yeah, emperors.

Spiritual DNA

And so long as you haven't experienced this,
to die and so to grow, you are only a troubled
guest on a dark earth.

Goethe

A SEED IS A PLANT IN ITS EMBRYONIC STAGE, protected by a shell. It's alive and intelligent and aware even when it looks like it's not, but until it transitions out of the shell and begins its growth stage, it's really just a state of stored potential. The same is true of the Human Child, but for reasons of nurture rather than nature, most human seedlings remain dormant until expiration, meaning that they never emerge from their shells and their potential goes unrealized. This is the fate of mankind, but it doesn't have to be the fate of you.

Within the herd, you are a single cell in a larger primary organism. It's not until you get a glimpse beyond the artificial context of the false self that you begin to see your true potential. It's only then that you understand the difference between being a small part of a larger organism or being a primary organism in your own right. Ideally and by design, you would undergo your second-stage birth transition from childhood to adulthood at the age of sexual maturity. Your life would then become a process of projecting your distinctive pattern – your spiritual DNA – outward into the creative medium of your dreamstate universe. The only way to find out what you really are is to become it, so if you never emerge from dormancy you'll never know who and what and where you really are, only the character you play.

❖

We have saviors who make big promises for what happens after you're dead – fat lotta good that does anyone – but what about the guy who saves you while you're still here in this life? The guy who tells you that you're only halfborn, that you're stuck in a dormant state in your juvenile seedcoat, that the life you're living is just meant to be a launchpad for the life you were born to live? The guy who tells you not only that there's a lot more to you, but how to actualize your potential? That guy sounds like the *real* savior, not the guy who saves you from his own demented father or tells you to sit in the middle of the road. Maybe we should concern ourselves less with after-life stuff and more with pre-death stuff. Maybe we should show some appreciation to the guy who helps us out here and now when it matters, not in some imagined future. Maybe a nice gift would be in order. I might have a few ideas on that subject.

❖

In physiology, the word *neoteny* refers to the condition of retaining juvenile characteristics into adulthood. Is there a psychological counterpart of neoteny? I can't spend my whole life hybridizing new terminology just to sound scientifical, but slapping the word spiritual on the front and adding initial caps usually works, so let's call the retention of juvenile mental and emotional characteristics into physical adulthood Spiritual Neoteny and see where it goes.

The trouble with Spiritual Neoteny is detecting it. If everyone suffered from it, then it would be normal and *not* suffering from it would make you an oddball. It's only by the presence of such oddballs that this condition could ever be detected, otherwise, we might never suspect that there was more to life than bestial survival and procreation. The guy who figured all this out – a *real* savior – should probably be sent a thank you note signed by everyone, maybe with a nice bottle of something. Or, if humanity were feeling particularly grateful, he might have his eye on a thirty-seven horsepower tractor with a few attachments. Used is okay, but since new equipment would only cost a smidge more, it might be a nice time to dig deep.

※

One thing you won't find when you depart from the beaten path and start finding your own way is all the assistance and resources you depend on in the herd. The road less traveled is not a road at all. There are no teachers or experts, no textbooks or field guides or maps. There are no clearly marked trails or well-worn ruts because you're not treading a path that billions have trod before. That's the nature of true discovery and exploration; you have to find your own way and travel light, pick up what you need and drop what you don't, make hard decisions and figure it out as you go. This may sound chaotic from the herd perspective where your whole life is mapped out cradle to grave, but when you become an adult, nothing is ever mapped out again; it's all trailblazing and bushwhacking and pioneering. You're all alone in an undiscovered country where you become whatever your newly unleashed spiritual DNA makes of you and you of it. Instead of books and schools and teachers, you learn to open your own channels of higher knowing and guidance in which needs are met as they arise. Instead of manmade rules and regulations, you discover lines of energetic flow and structure. Right-knowing and right-action become your new modes of navigation.

The cocreative dreamstate becomes both your playground and playmate. This is what your adulthood would be like if you ever got there. This is the life that has been taken from you and replaced with mindless child-rearing, money-earning, pleasure-seeking, and role-playing. I don't know if you know what a grapple is, but it's like a hydraulic steel mouth on the front of a tractor that can grab logs and brush and haul it around. I bet humanity's in-life savior would really appreciate one of those.

❖

When seeds know they're in a hostile place, they remain safe inside the shell. When they know they're in a warm, moist, sunny place, they emerge from the shell and, with a little luck and grit, begin the journey of fulfilling their potential. Right now, you are stuck in your shell because the herd is a nonconducive growth medium in which germination cannot occur. Unlike your herdmates however, you are not content in your dormant state, which we know because here you are. Good for you. Still, we can't ignore the fact that you are well past your due date, which raises an interesting question: Are you still viable? And the answer to that all-important question is…

Maybe.

We know that belated emergence is possible because that's the only kind we ever see. The transition to adulthood never takes place in its natural timeframe.

Blame this aberration on the self-propagating nature of fear. We pull our children in tight just as we were pulled in tight and just as they'll pull their children in tight. We call this constrictive behavior loving, but the source of love in its negative aspect is fear, and that's the only kind an eyes-closed, fear-based human child is capable of. It's the nature of fear to grab and hold and protect, whereas it's the nature of trust to surrender and release and allow. Love in its negative aspect is clingy and mawkish – selective and personal and egoic – but in its defense, that's where we get all the good songs. In its positive aspect, love is impersonal and unconditional; I love you because I love creation and being and dogs and drama, and even stuff I don't like, like ego and snapping turtles and Skittles. Humanity dwells in the dungeon of fear and gloms on to its children so they are likewise damned. Ideally, parents should sacrifice themselves to raise their kids up and out of these conditions, but juvenile parents aspire only for their children to become next-gen versions of themselves. What better way of pledging your allegiance to the herd than offering up your children for sacrifice on the altar of groupthink, orthodoxy, and mindless conformity? That's what life is for virtually everyone you've ever known, but it doesn't have to be that way for you...

Maybe.

For the same reason, it's not true that humanity is evolving. It always changes but never improves. In fact, a much stronger case can be made that we are devolving; that as science and technology and medicine move forward, humanity moves back. As long as we remain eyes-closed, fear-based, halfborn and herdbound, what claim to evolution can we possibly make? We fancy ourselves bold explorers of the unknown, but our inner dimensions remain strictly off-limits; what Alan Watts called the taboo against knowing who you are. As long as we remain slaves to manipulation and control in every area of our lives, in what possible sense are we an improvement on our forebears? As long as we're stuck playing these two-dimensional roles in this done-to-death drama, there's no chance of enlivening the broader dimensions of our personal potential. It's not until you make the transition from juvenile to adult that your life becomes new and original, like nothing yet dreamed of. Sure, it's still the dreamstate, it's still false context, but now it's *your* context determined by *your* spiritual DNA, and that does not appear in any book but the one *you* write. We think that making money and having kids is the best we can do, but the creative expression of our unique pattern is the adventure that awaits us, and *that's* the best we can do.

Can you emerge from this juvenile paradigm? Can you make the transition from small, dark dungeon to openness and light? From fear to surrender? Can you make the polar shift from love-negative to love-positive? Maybe. Mind is the sword and heart is the will to use it. If you can bring both mind and heart into focused alignment, you can make the transition from juvenile to adult and begin your authentic life, but that's a pretty big if. Life in the shell is the only life you've ever known, so to emerge means to die from one existence and, with a little luck and grit, be born into another. There's no overstating the death part, but you can find courage in your own mortality. Let death be your open ally instead of a hidden enemy and you can turn the odds in your favor, but regardless of whether or not you accept this invitation, I would think a front-mounted plow and a rear-mounted mower deck would go without saying.

❖

As we see wherever we look, the vast majority of human seedlings fail to germinate. They never emerge from the juvenile shell and never take root in the growth medium of the cocreative dreamstate. Those that do emerge will develop into the living expression of their own unique potential, so that's what I wonder when I look at people. Who are you? Who would you be if you became who you really are? What tremendous and unique potential is curled up inside your shell? Even now, you don't really believe me. The way I know you don't believe me is because if you did, you'd be screaming and thrashing and peeling off your skin and jumping into volcanoes and doing whatever it took to reboot your human operating system and bring your mission-critical functions back online. You *can't* believe me because it's not a matter of believing but of opening your eyes and seeing. In the segregated state, your potential is severely restricted, but in the integrated state, you are certain to become something new and unprecedented, something we don't even have the words or concepts to describe. What we *do* have the words and concepts to describe is the box-grader, which is a big help in making and tending woodland trails and gravel roads, and they're pretty affordable. Not to go on about it, but if everyone pitched in, the per-person out-of-pocket contribution to the Global In-Life Savior Appreciation Tractor Fund would be roughly a thousandth of a cent. That seems pretty doable, especially compared to what post-life saviors get. I'll start us off with a dollar; that should cover myself and Fiji.

◆

I'm not selling the integrated state, I'm just trying to do an adequate job of portraying it. Once you understand it, adulthood sells itself. Everything you want in life, all your spiritual desires – your wish to find yourself, to discover your purpose and your own personal meaning, to access and fulfill your potential, to experience unconditional love, to create and shape your own reality – can only be found when you make the transition from child to adult. You can't achieve your purpose or express your potential within the juvenile shell; only by sprouting and manifesting yourself can you ever know who and what and where you are. This is what everyone really wants from spirituality, but it comes at a price which, from the child side of the equation, looks like everything. That's the gateless gate thing, and the only way to understand it is to pass through and see that the price was really nothing all along.

The birth of the plant marks the death of the seed. What the caterpillar calls the end of the world, the rest of the world calls a butterfly. That Goethe quote at the top of the chapter is from a poem called *The Holy Longing*, which contains these words:

> I praise what is truly alive, what
> longs to be burned to death.

Your Little Bastard is that part of you that understands exactly what Goethe meant, and that's why you keep that part of yourself buried under a mountain of emotional debris. He's the voice of the inner black hole summoning you beyond the illusion of selfhood. You might hear him as an unhealthy self-destructive impulse, but he's really your one true guru, so if you want to wake up and find your life, you're gonna have to dig him up and hear him out. And while you're at it, see if he says anything about a hydraulic backhoe attachment. *Super* handy.

Adult Utopia

Our descendants will sooner or later reach, as a
race, the condition of cosmic consciousness, just
as, long ago, our ancestors passed from simple
consciousness into self consciousness.

R.M. Bucke, Cosmic Consciousness

A YOUNG MAN RAISES HIS HAND to ask a question.
I nod and he starts talking about himself; his
story, his circumstances, his experiences, his feelings,
his beliefs, his spiritual history. I won't try repeating
what he said because I don't care and neither should
he and neither should you. None of that personal crap
matters. Awakening in or from the dreamstate is an
impersonal process, and all that biographical baggage
amounts to nothing more than the debris with which
we conceal, mask and distract from the only thing that
does matter, which is making it to and through the
black hole within; the only spiritual path there is.

It's surprising how often people mistake this process for housekeeping instead of arson. I'm pretty sure that if you start telling a Roshi about your feelings, you're gonna get a taste of the stick. I wouldn't hit students with a stick for asking dumb questions because it seems like too much bother. Like, is there an etiquette or protocol? Do I have to get up and come over to you? What if you flinch and I don't get a clean shot, do I get a do-over? A mulligan? How many tries do I get? Or do you approach me to get hit? How does that get conveyed to you? Is there a gesture or a command I'm supposed to give, or does anyone who talks to me have to come within hitting distance first? What's that, like three feet? I don't want anyone within *ten* feet of me. And what if you're one of those people who *like* to get whacked? That could get pretty weird pretty fast. The whole stick-hitting thing sounds like more trouble than it's worth, but I could see where a phaser set on stun, mostly, might solve a lot of these problems. I could blast whoever I want and they'd just take a little timeout and be okay, mostly, within a few hours. I'm sure the first twenty pages of the phaser instruction manual would contain bold red warnings like "Never point at people or animals!", "Can cause blindness, brain damage, paralysis, or death!", "If hit by phaser, seek immediate medical treatment!", and all that paranoid legal junk, so I'd probably have to get special insurance and have students sign waivers absolving me in advance for any physical and emotional scarring, post-spiritual stress disorder, melted fillings, light-to-medium scorching, and bladder-control issues. I guess the Roshis have it pretty easy, or maybe they just have good lawyers.

❖

People in group settings try to kill time by asking me questions about myself as a person – lifestyle, writing habits, views on current events, Mac or PC, crunchy or creamy – but the only significant thing about me is my function. I am an apple tree. I produce fruit. You may like apples or not, but you don't stand around making small talk with the tree. I ignore their personal questions and turn their attention back where it belongs.

"It's not *me* that should be interesting to you, it's *you*. You should totally blow your mind. Every one of you should find yourself to be far and away the most magnificent, amazing, remarkable thing in creation. That's not make-real, happy-time ass-talk, that's absolutely how you should look at yourself and your fleeting moment of in-character awareness and cocreative partnership. If you're not the single greatest miracle of creation by your own reckoning, then you're not paying attention. This goes right to the heart of all this awakening and spiritual stuff. Make a real effort to open your eyes and understand who and what and where you really are. When you think of yourself as just one more cow in an endless herd it doesn't sound so special, but that's not what you really are, that's just the lie that's been burned into you like a brand. When you're asleep you see yourself as just another cell in a huge organism made up of billions of similar cells, but when you open your eyes and see for yourself, you discover that you're singular and unique; *sui generis*, a class of your own. You are not a part of a larger being but a full and complete being in your own right, and you're the only one of your kind.

"You've been brainwashed by the promise of heaven and reincarnation and immortality to live your life as if it goes on forever and there's no urgency, but the urgency is real and you're already late to the party. You have a small window of time to wake up and figure out what's going on. You are consciousness and the universe is consciousness, no difference. You are a point of awareness with a body for a vehicle and a planet for a playground in a timespace energymatter reality, but this setup doesn't last forever. The truth is that you are the diamond heart of awareness at the center of your own personal universe; how is that not the coolest thing ever? What could possibly be more amazing to you than you? Not what came before but what might lie ahead. Not what you are right now but what you might become. I have no idea what your potential is, but more importantly, neither do you. I don't mean potential like you might get a degree or run for office or become a priest or the head of a drug cartel, I mean that you could do things in the realm of emotionally-powered cocreative intelligence that you'll need a new vocabulary to describe. You could go somewhere that doesn't appear on any map and become something no one has ever dreamed of. Compare that potential with the life you're living now which is probably so tightly-scripted and rigidly defined as to be hardly worth getting out of bed for. Feel free to be offended, by the way; if truth hurts then pain is your friend. If you could see the difference between your juvenile reality and your adult potential, you'd have no other thought than to make that transition regardless of any other consideration. The reason you don't live in a state of constant total amazement is not because it's not constantly totally amazing, but because you're constantly totally asleep, and I guess you agree which is why you're here instead of with any of the countless New Age smoke-blowers and ass-talkers who tell you to sit down, shut up and close your eyes; to be mellow and find peace in your confinement. I'm not saying you should turn into a total dipshit about it, I'm saying that if you take your situation for granted and waste your life as just another cow in the herd, then you're *already* a total dipshit. Again, feel free to be offended, but point your anger in the right direction. Don't waste it on me. You may be the victim of this crime, but you're also very much the criminal."

I pause and take a drink of oversweet lemonade and discretely spit it out before continuing.

"By my estimate, we only have a few viable years — something in the twenty-six to thirty-four age range — during which we can marshal sufficient mental focus, emotional energy, and physical stamina to bring about change, to retrace every step back to the beginning and start over in the right direction. That's basically the map of the death-rebirth process; the undoing of negative progress being the death part and setting out in a positive direction being rebirth. They don't tell you about that in the spiritual marketplace because their success depends on assuring eyes-closed, fear-based, halfborn people that their eyes are open and that they're capable of great spiritual things. They tell us that where we are now is just fine, that our beliefs and assumptions are all valid and correct, that all we have to do is learn some stuff and practice some techniques and have a nice little epiphany and we'll win the big spiritual prize and be the envy of family and friends and live happily ever after. That's what we want to hear — that it's all rebirth and no death — and that's what they tell us because the spiritual marketplace isn't truth-driven or results-driven, it's consumer-driven. In this sense, it's no different from anything else in the dreamstate. All ministries serve the opposite of their stated purpose, and the Ministry of Awakening is no exception.

"I am a point of awareness looking out from inside this physical vehicle onto a surrounding dreamstate reality. This character I play is like a rental car to me and this dreamstate is like a motel. I have no real connection to it, no pride of ownership, no sense of permanence or belonging. That's the reality of you too, but you're so caught up in the illusion of selfhood that you can't distinguish passenger from vehicle or guest from motel. We're all just finite units of infinite awareness. We gather bits of debris and combine our flotsam with neighboring jetsam to form islands and archipelagos and continents. We find company and connection in these ramshackle floating structures, but no configuration of emotional rubbish can change the fact that we are each alone on a shoreless sea.

"Awareness is perfectly impersonal. There's no *my* awareness or *your* awareness, there's only awareness itself. The truth of you and the truth of Buddha, Hitler, Stalin, and Christ is the same truth. All truth is one truth, all consciousness is one consciousness, and that thou art. Once we release our desperate hold on the accumulated detritus of selfhood and allow ourselves to sink beneath the surface, two things happen; first *dis*integration, then *re*integration. We recede from personal appearance and proceed into impersonal awareness. This is the one and only spiritual path; everything else is about maintaining and reinforcing the illusion of selfhood. We become attached to ego primarily and the world secondarily. Self and other. First and foremost we attach to the person we find ourselves to be – body, mind, thoughts, feelings – then, that core self becomes the hub for all the countless attachments we pick up as we go. The process of awakening from delusion entails the severing of these attachments progressively; weakest to strongest. This process is self-regulating and once it starts, all we can do is hold on and try to survive from one downsizing to the next. It takes a year or two, it's painful, it sucks, but eventually you come to the kill-the-Buddha moment when you confront the mother of all attachments; self itself. This is the war we wage when we confront the black hole within, but now it all comes down to the final conflict and there are only two warriors left standing; fear of no-self and hatred of false self. The real war is about destroying the illusion that there was ever a self or a dreamstate in the first place, so in the end, no one is left standing and no one wins. In other words, the greatest trick Maya ever pulled was convincing the world that she exists."

❖

I shut up and let the conversation pick up around me. I get a bunch of questions that feel like sidestreets and deadends so I just kind of smile and shrug and ignore them until someone asks if there could ever be a utopian, adult-based society. That's better. I've played with this idea and concluded that it could work in theory but not in practice.

"In an adult society, we wouldn't be discussing escape from the dungeon because we wouldn't have gotten locked up in the first place. You wouldn't mistake the segregated state for a permanent condition so you wouldn't form an unhealthy attachment to your juvenile character. Rather than a belated, self-instigated transition in your twenties or thirties, you'd undergo a timely, natural transition at the age of sexual maturity. Being raised by adults, your youth would be spent exploring and discovering and finding your own way in the world. Your inner black hole would not be buried under a mountain of emotional debris, it would be sitting out in the open, waiting for you to make a healthy transition from the sandbox of the child to the unlimited cocreative playspace of the adult. As an adult, your time and lifeforce wouldn't be wasted on the denial of no-self and projection of false-self, so they could be put to much better use. You'd have an open and honest relationship with your own mortality so you wouldn't have to fabricate and inhabit a fairytale narrative to shield you from truth.

"An adult society would be much less cohesive than the juvenile herd. Remove the gravity well of fear and everyone would naturally drift apart. Such a society would not need a shared false-narrative to provide meaning and context because alignment with your own unique spiritual DNA provides all the meaning and context you need. The meaning would still be artificial because all art is artifice and your life is your work of art. The context would still be false because all games are false and your life is just a game you play.

Understood correctly – directly, honestly, fearlessly – what need could there be for fabrication and lies?

"I'm on my journey, you're on yours, and maybe once a month we meet at the farmer's market and swap stories about how you've learned to raise and shape massive stones with your voice and how I've learned to channel the goddess of illusion. We'd share our experiences while you gave me a haircut and I repaired your shoes. That's probably when savage hordes would ride in from distant lands and cut off our heads, burn our homes, steal our children and reestablish an eyes-closed, fear-based society, but our adult-based utopia would have been nice while it lasted.

"The big difference would be kids. The parent-child bond would look very different in an adult society; still powerful but less possessive and needy. In an adult society, children would not be used to plug the inner black holes of the parents by creating the illusion of meaning, context and purpose, as they are now. How do you raise someone to become a Human Adult? Through non-interference, release, trust. By letting nature take its course. By pushing them out of the nest at the appropriate time to fly or die. You teach them to read, write and reckon, give them access to a library, and then when the time comes, kick them out and wish them well. Maybe not quite that heavy on the tough-love, but close.

"We accept that going to school, getting a job, getting married and having kids is the highest ideal to which we might aspire, that retirement and grandkids are the rewards for a life well-lived, that shuffling cradle-to-grave like mindless drones is the path of the righteous, but if you're just one cow in an endless herd, then in what sense are you anything more than a commodity? If you can be replaced like a lightbulb, then you're just an interchangeable part. In the expression of our spiritual DNA, we are all unique; no one is replaceable or interchangeable. However many snowflakes might exist, each one forms the nucleus of its own dreamstate universe. No snowflake can ever come again and no two can ever be the same. In one sense, what you become while you're here doesn't matter, in another sense, it's the only thing that does.

"Imagine how your life might be different if you'd spent your early years in a nurturing, growth-conducive environment instead of being sentenced to rot in government storage facilities, if you'd been raised by adults to become an adult instead of sitting in classrooms hour after week after month after year, learning and discovering nothing of value, accomplishing nothing more than the systematic disposal of your formative years, and therefore, your life. Most of the spirit-neutering, mind-numbing garbage we're force-fed in school wouldn't even exist as subject matter in an adult society and might be replaced by weird-sounding subjects like Wei Wu Wei, Cocreative Integration, Dreamstate Reality, Transpersonal Navigation, and Subtle Energy Dynamics, but even those would be as unnecessary as classes in Standing, Walking and Running are today. You'd master these subjects as easily and naturally as you mastered your mother tongue. What might any of us become if we found our direction early and followed it through life? What are we really capable of? That's what the question of an adult utopia really boils down to; not what are *people* capable of or what is a *person* capable of, but what *you* are capable of? What might any of us become in this life given an upbringing that was *not* in violation of the natural order, raised by people who were *not* themselves morbidly obtuse in a society that *wasn't* fanatically devoted to the crushing of the human spirit? Imagine what your life might have been had all forces *not* conspired against you."

❖

Speaking in my capacity as an apple tree, somewhere around the age of thirty I underwent a radical course correction and have since followed a fixed outbound trajectory. These books I write are the record of my journey, brought into focus and refinement through the writing and editing process itself. I go where my course takes me and I use the externalized thought process of writing to make sense of it as I go. What does an apple tree do? It takes what it needs from the soil, air, sky, and the perfect intelligence that informs all things, and through some weird alchemy, it turns all that into an apple. Same with me, only books.

As I said early on, I didn't receive the Total Knowledge Package with this enlightenment deal, so what I know is what I've figured out for myself and much of it has come as a surprise. When I started writing the books twenty years ago, I thought my topic was waking from the dreamstate – enlightenment – but I soon learned that one or two books were more than enough on that subject and that my unique trajectory was becoming more about waking *in* the dreamstate – adulthood – and here we are in my tenth book. "Camerado, this is no book," said Whitman, "who touches this touches a man." You can say I'm just another New Age hack cultivating my reflection in the eyes of readers, or you can look from a higher perspective and see me not as a person but a function; I am an apple tree and I exist to produce this particular fruit. I act, but I don't reflect on the fruit of my act, and by my fruit shall ye know me. Does that mean my books are pure truth handed down from on high? No, maybe it's all lies and bullshit. Maybe instead of apples I'm producing stinky assfruit and by my fruit you know me as a stinky asstree. I don't think that's the case, but even if it were, that would be my function and I'd perform it. Obviously we're not limited to only creating good, honest, morally upright fruit. The universe doesn't care *what* we create, only that we *do*.

Once you set out on a straight-line trajectory, you have no idea where your journey will take you. Maybe you begin as a painter and that evolves into inventing some new class of artwork based on the atmosphere instead of paint; setting the aurora borealis to music or composing thunderstorms, but still with further to go. I have no idea what anyone might become or what fruit they might bear, I simply believe that anyone can find their outbound trajectory and follow it as far as they're able and that no two journeys will produce the same discoveries or yield the same creative output. What might Thoreau have become had he not died in his forties? Was he really a naturalist, or was that just his early course? Where might his trajectory have taken him given another thirty or forty years? Jim Morrison might have gone far beyond poetry and music if he'd had the chance. Who knows? No one knows anything – I certainly don't – but that's the nature of the dreamstate. Obviously, we're here to play and create and explore, not walk in circles, eating, mooing and mating, blinded by our own dustcloud and imprisoned by fear... Wait, scratch that. Obviously, that *is* why most of us are here since that's what most of us do, but maybe you can do something different.

If I write another book, I'll call it *Jed Talks 4: Beauty Enough to Stop a War*. In it, I'll take a break from criticizing eyes-closed, fear-based humanity and start singing its praises. I'll try to express the true magnificence and wonder and complexity of the dramatic dreamstate, and the infinite consciousness and perfect intelligence underlying it. We kings and slaves, sages and scholars, artists and warriors and kids of all ages have mounted and manned this diverse, long-running, theatrical production, and one of the benefits of awakening from the spectacle – the *un*suspension of disbelief – is the ability to view it in the new light of detachment. I see all this from the enlightened perspective, which you might not like as much as you'd like. You'll love it when you're here beside me, but you won't like hearing it described from where you are. You won't agree that the horror-and-suffering end of the experiential spectrum is just as perfect and wondrous and beautiful as the love-and-beauty end. That's a tough cross-paradigm sell, but what are we doing here if not elevating and expanding our perspective? *You must learn to see with the same eye a mound of earth and a heap of gold, a cow and a sage, a dog and the man who eats the dog.* I'm not suggesting that you *feel* that stomach cancer is the same as a basket of puppies, but there is a perspective from which they're exactly the same, and that must be what you're here to see because that's where all this leads.

We look through the filters of preference and bias and emotional discrimination, but we can flip those filters out of the way and see with naked, unaided, uncorrupted eye. You don't have to form preferences and take sides and judge everything you behold, you can just look, just see, just sit back and wonder at the mystery and majesty of this production; not as a player on the stage but as a spectator in the nosebleed seats from where you can't tell good guys from bad guys because from this altitude, all the players look like ants, which is, of course, what we really are.

Life is about creation. The creative process is fully scalable; the same process that weaves a basket into being weaves galaxies into being. The point of creation is creation; it is an end in itself, and whether you consider yourself creative or not, you are a part of creation, no more or less than any other. *The powerful play goes on, and you will contribute a verse.* A tree that does not produce a fruit may itself be the fruit; they also serve who only fill out the forest. Even if you're not starting wars or writing symphonies or building a better mousetrap, you're as much a part of the grand dramatic spectacle as those who swing the swords and sing the arias.

If you gave me a million dollars, I'd buy a tractor and some attachments and stick the rest in my sock drawer and forget it's there. If you gave me a child I'd give it back. If the Nobel committee called, I'd change my number. I have all the purpose and meaning I need right here in my own private dreamstate. I have my health, I know my function, and I see my path forward. That's the goal of spirituality, the realization of the Taoist ideal, and the only adult utopia we can ever hope to find.

Goddess III:
Soft & Yielding

YIN

Okay Maestro, we're on a roll, let's keep it going.

YANG

Yeah, this Tao thing sounds pretty great.

LAO TZU

Well, no, it's not that it's *great*. That's really where they get you. You can't really say it's great or not great, or this or not that, see what I mean? The infinite cannot be captured by the finite, right? The Tao is kind of like everything and the only thing, so anything you say about it is necessarily incorrect.

YANG

Or maybe everything you say about it is *super*-correct.

YIN

Yeah, I like that better. Less negative.

YANG

I know, right? More accessible. We have to keep the common man in mind here.

YIN

Yeah, the Tao shouldn't be a downer.

YANG

Oh good one! Write that!

LAO TZU

No, don't write that. Look, as soon as you dilute the truth even just the teensiest little bit…

YIN

Yeah, we get it. Listen, I'm gonna write it down the way we said and we can come back to it later. We just want to get you out of here before winter sets in or you'll be here 'til spring. We'll wrap up with you and send you on your way, then we can tidy up the paperwork. Sound good?

LAO TZU

Well, I'm starting to feel like this might be my legacy, my gift to the world, and…

YANG

Whoa, pump the brakes there, buddy. One minute you're leaving the country, and now you're leaving gifts to the world?

LAO TZU

Well, you got me excited about our little project.

YIN

It's a form, not a project.

YANG

Yeah Maestro, we're not your devoted pupils or your muse, we're just a couple of guys who made some bad life choices and now we're stuck in this shack playing Pinky Touch for months at a time.

YIN

Let's try to reign in our expectations, shall we?

The door bursts open and an old lady enters.

YANG

You got laundry?

OLD LADY

You got ticky?

YANG

No ticky.

OLD LADY

So solly. No ticky, no laundry.

YIN

Yeah, this never gets old.

OLD LADY

slaps Yin on back of head

Aw, you boys are no fun.

She steps out and returns with a basket of folded clothes. Sees Lao Tzu.

OLD LADY

Who's this guy?

YIN

Venerable Master.

OLD LADY

Is that your water buffalo parked outside?

LAO TZU

That's my Bubby.

OLD LADY

Oh, I know you! I saw you once. You were giving a talk in a tea house. You said we should all be more like water. We thought you were drunk.

LAO TZU

Could be. I went through a dark period...

OLD LADY

You told a story about a man whose horse ran away and everyone was sad for him, but he just said, "We'll see."

LAO TZU

I don't think that was me.

OLD LADY

Then his horse came back with a bunch of other horses and everyone was happy for the man, and he said, "We'll see."

LAO TZU

Yeah, I know the story.

OLD LADY

And then the man's son breaks his leg on one of the new horses and everyone is sad for the man...

YIN

And he just says "We'll see."

YANG

Does it just go on like this?

LAO TZU

It goes on forever.

OLD LADY

And then they come to make the son a soldier for war, but his leg is broken so they can't take him, and...

YANG

Everyone is happy for the man.

YIN

Yeah, I think we get it.

OLD LADY

Well, at the tea house, he went on for like ten more things; happy, sad, happy, sad, we'll see, we'll see, we'll see.

YIN

And what's the point?

OLD LADY

Be like water, I guess.

YANG

to Lao Tzu

Is that the point? Be like water?

LAO TZU

I don't remember, I was going through some stuff...

OLD LADY

The man in the story is supposed to be wise because he doesn't have highs and lows, he's always level like water.

YANG

That sounds dumb. What's wrong with highs and lows?

YIN

Yeah, if my best horse ran away, I'd be like, really bummed.

YANG

And if it came back with a bunch of others, I'd be like, *wahoo!*

OLD LADY

That's what we thought at the tea house, like the man sounded pretty boring. No ups and downs, always just flat.

LAO TZU

Water always finds its own level, it follows the path of least resistance, it's humble, it dwells in the lowest places. It's like, you know, an allegory.

OLD LADY

You have any new material since then?

LAO TZU

I'm not a stand-up comic, I'm a sage, a wise man.

YANG

A venerable master.

LAO TZU

Exactly. Well, that's my name, but...

OLD LADY

So you're on tour? Cheering up the troops?

LAO TZU

Not really, I'm uh...

YANG

He's leaving China.

OLD LADY

Leaving China? What kind of bullshit is that? Where you going?

LAO TZU

Nowhere really, just off to live in nature.

OLD LADY

What, there's not enough nature here for you? This place is *all* nature, the whole country, nothing but nature, everywhere you look, nature, up the yinyang...

YIN & YANG

Hey!

OLD LADY

...and you gotta leave because some other place has better nature?

LAO TZU

I don't know, I'm just looking for a change of scenery.

OLD LADY

Is that what water does? Look for a change of scenery?

LAO TZU

I don't think you really get the whole water thing.

YIN

We're making him write down his wisdom before he goes.

YANG

In case it's any good.

OLD LADY

It doesn't sound very good. That guy with the horses sounds like a real jerk.

YANG

Yeah, someone should give that guy a good karate chop!

YIN

Kung fu.

YANG

Yeah, a good kung fu chop!

LAO TZU

Well, it's not really a real person.

YIN

What, you just made the whole story up?

YANG

Is that a wiseman thing? Making up stories?

LAO TZU

Yeah, kind of. It's an allegory, a parable.

YANG

He can't just say be like water, he has to make up a whole story.

OLD LADY

Okay, what else you got, Mr. Wisdom?

YIN

He said those who know don't talk and those who talk don't know.

OLD LADY

Know what?

YIN

He didn't say.

OLD LADY

Does that mean he knows or not?

YIN

Don't know.

YANG

Become master of the universe without striving, he said.

OLD LADY

to Lao Tzu

Are you master of the universe?

LAO TZU

It's not like it sounds.

OLD LADY

It sounds like master of the universe. Is that what you are?

LAO TZU

Yes and no.

OLD LADY

Does the universe do your bidding?

LAO TZU

Yes and no.

OLD LADY

More yes or more no?

LAO TZU

More no but some yes. I like to focus on the yes.

OLD LADY

Is it doing your bidding right now? Getting you stuck in this dump?

LAO TZU

Well, what the universe wants and what I want are really the same thing, so I guess the answer is yes. If this is what the universe wants, I want it too, even if I don't understand it right now.

OLD LADY

That's a little convenient, don't you think?

LAO TZU

It is convenient, yes.

YANG

So if we throw him off a cliff, he'll just be like, okay, I'm at one with the universe because I like getting thrown off cliffs all the time.

OLD LADY

So then maybe I'm a wise man too since I'm in this shack doing the bidding of the universe, right?

LAO TZU

Technically, that would be correct. You are really just an isolated energetic pattern in a vast ocean of energy, so your experience is one of either alignment or misalignment with the currents of being. I live in alignment with the current and flow, so my experience of life is smooth and effortless. If your experience of life is not smooth and effortless, then that's a reflection of your misalignment with the primal energy and overarching intelligence, the Tao.

OLD LADY

to Yin

Holy shit! That was good! Did you write that down? I think there might be a book in this!

YIN

We just need to fill in the form.

OLD LADY

No, seriously, this guy talks real wise. We squeeze a bestseller out of him and, you know, we're all outta here. Champagne wishes and caviar dreams, right?

YIN

Are you sure he's wise? I thought he was just pulling our yangs.

YANG

Hey!

OLD LADY

Old man, say something wise.

LAO TZU

I do nothing, yet nothing goes undone.

OLD LADY

Bingo! That's exactly the kind of crap we're looking for.

LAO TZU

It's not crap, it's real wisdom. It's a real way to live and if people understand that they can lead lives of greater ease and comfort.

OLD LADY

Yeah, no shit. If people buy our book, *I* can live a life of greater ease and comfort. I don't know if you've ever had to wash clothes in a frigid river or perform sex acts on a couple of Mongoloids...

YANG

aside to Yin

Did she just insult us?

YIN

aside to Yang

Surprisingly, no.

OLD LADY

...but I can tell you, it leaves a lot to be desired. Is this wisdom of yours some big whoop? Great, but so is having a bestseller and getting rich and giving these poor old knees a rest. You wanna say some clever stuff like you don't do anything and everything still gets done, that's good for both of us. You sound wise and we get rich. That, or we eat your buffalo and throw you off a cliff. Your choice.

LAO TZU

Do I still get to have my name on the book?

OLD LADY

If it's between Venerable Master or Elderly Prostitute, which do you think is gonna zoom up the charts?

Marichelle 8:
Trouble Is Fine

Right from the start, all your ideas are wrong, so that's not good. If you are not happy about this, you can either get happy or change your ideas. I'm not sure which is better.

*

Talking to me will make a mess for you where you wanted everything to be very nice and have a nice time. If you want to have a nice time you're in the wrong place. Talking to me will only make things worse.

*

We like to think we are very brave, or maybe brave enough, but we're really not too brave. That's not a bad thing, it's just a thing. For this you don't need to *have* bravery, you have to *find* bravery. You don't know what brave is yet, but it's in you.

✳

This is all the way. There is no part way. I think that's where you get confused. It's either all the way or none of the way. It's not like other things. With this, even most of the way is still none of the way.

✳

You can understand everything, all you have to do is look. I can point for you, but you have to look. It's harder than it sounds or everyone would do it instead of almost no one.

✳

You worry about leaving somewhere and going nowhere but it's really the other way. It sounds like I'm saying different things but I'm just saying the same thing over and over. It's okay to be confused at this point, I would say.

✳

The reason I'm knitting is because I like to knit when I talk. I also like to knit when I don't talk. I like to knit a lot of the time. Knitting makes one part of my brain be quiet so another part can do other things. That's how it seems anyway.

*

You should maybe try knitting. I think everyone would like it. I recommend it as a spiritual thing to do, like a meditation or something. I can go all over the place when I'm knitting even though I'm right here. I get a lot done when I knit.

*

You're here and we're talking and I'm knitting. If you weren't here we wouldn't be talking but I would still be knitting. I can knit and talk or I can just knit. This is something all the world leaders should do when they sit around their big tables. I think they'd start less trouble that way. Just kidding, trouble is fine.

*

The way everything is now is fine. It's a system so it works a certain way, right? If we look at how it works we can understand it. Maybe it's a mystery because we don't look. Maybe we don't understand because we don't look, but we can look if we want to. It's just sitting there.

*

Here's some good news for you. Whatever spiritual things you do you can stop doing. Keep doing them if you want to, but not for this. They don't do anything for this, more like the opposite because you think you're doing something when you're not, so nothing ever gets done. It can be a little tricky.

*

For me, knitting is a spiritual thing, but it doesn't go anywhere. It's like a spiritual thing for me, but not because it does anything. Maybe I start knitting in the morning and the whole day goes by, but then I get up right where I sat down.

*

No one is looking for truth, that's just talk. Truth doesn't hide from us, we hide from truth. If you have to look for truth, you won't find it because it's always right where you never look. It's like a trick you play on yourself, looking all over for something you already have.

*

Maybe you just want to chase after something. Maybe we really want something or maybe we just want to chase something. It's something to do. It's nice to have something to chase, even if it's just in circles.

*

Maybe we think we can do something, like get somewhere or become something. That's what makes us go but that's not how it is. It's not like you go, it's like you come back, like you make a big circle and come back. Maybe everything is circles. I can't decide right now.

*

There's no great other place to get to. You're better off if you can just figure out where you are. Being in coma is enough to worry about. Try getting out of coma and then see where you are. You might be pretty surprised. You might want to go right back into coma.

*

When you're religious, you want to be in deeper sleep, be less awake, right? That's what it is. You want to have a nice quiet time. You want to be less scared so you can be more happy. Why make it a bad thing if that's what you want? Be less scared, more happy. Why not?

*

Don't make religion bad. Religion is part of the system. The system needs religion. Maybe the system *is* religion, or religion is just another name for the system. I don't think there's much difference.

✳

You can be religious and talk about truth but they're two different things. You might think they're the same but they're practically the opposite. If you want religion you can say anything is true and no one can argue with you. If you want truth you won't spend much time being religious.

✳

Even when we're not religious we're still very religious. When you think you're not religious, it just means you don't have a good idea what religion is. It's not just this one thing like God and all that, it's more like everything. It's really everywhere so it can be very hard to see.

✳

Everyone is really the same religion but no one knows what it is. You don't even know your own religion, which is pretty funny. We like to think we're these very smart people, but we're just little monkeys.

The Folly of Human Conceits

*In 1990, at the request of author and astronomer Carl
Sagan, NASA instructed the outbound Voyager I
space probe to take a picture of our planet from 3.76
billion miles away. The resulting photo shows Earth as
one tiny speck among millions of tiny specks. The
following is from a speech Sagan gave at Cornell in
1994.*

WE SUCCEEDED IN TAKING THAT PICTURE,
and, if you look at it, you see a dot. That's
here. That's home. That's us. On it, everyone you ever
heard of, every human being who ever lived, lived
out their lives. The aggregate of all our joys and suf-
ferings, thousands of confident religions, ideologies
and economic doctrines, every hunter and forager,
every hero and coward, every creator and destroyer
of civilizations, every king and peasant, every young
couple in love, every hopeful child, every mother and
father, every inventor and explorer, every teacher of
morals, every corrupt politician, every superstar, every
supreme leader, every saint and sinner in the history of
our species, lived there on a mote of dust, suspended
in a sunbeam.

The Earth is a very small stage in a vast cosmic arena. Think of the rivers of blood spilled by all those generals and emperors so that in glory and in triumph they could become the momentary masters of a fraction of a dot. Think of the endless cruelties visited by the inhabitants of one corner of the dot on scarcely distinguishable inhabitants of some other corner of the dot. How frequent their misunderstandings, how eager they are to kill one another, how fervent their hatreds. Our posturings, our imagined self-importance, the delusion that we have some privileged position in the universe, are challenged by this point of pale light.

Our planet is a lonely speck in the great enveloping cosmic dark. In our obscurity – in all this vastness – there is no hint that help will come from elsewhere to save us from ourselves. It is up to us. It's been said that astronomy is a humbling, and I might add, a character-building experience. To my mind, there is perhaps no better demonstration of the folly of human conceits than this distant image of our tiny world.

The Tao of Self-Annihilation

We have to continually be jumping off cliffs
and developing our wings on the way down.

Kurt Vonnegut

"START YOUR INQUIRY LIKE a journalist," I reply
when asked about spiritual autolysis by a young
lady of college-age. There's a small group casually
gathered around me asking questions, and this is one
I'm happy to answer.

"Put all your knowledge and assumptions aside and
start fresh. Who are you? What and where are you?
Why are you? What do you know for sure? Start with
a blank page and find your question or let your question find you. It all boils down to self-inquiry – asking
Who am I? – but you don't have to jump into the deep
end. Start with something simple and let the process
follow its own course.

"The process is simple and natural, but don't let ego or vanity push you away. When you sense resistance, turn into it. When you sense bullshit, attack it. When you feel fear, go into it. When you stumble into darkness, light it up. When you write, puke all your messy, stupid, crazy thoughts and beliefs out onto the page. Make a promise to yourself that you'll burn or delete everything you write so you can express yourself honestly without fear of judgment or ridicule. Once you start, it can come gushing out. Don't hold back. Don't edit yourself for public consumption; this isn't a journal to share with your shrink or a diary your mom might see. It might seem brilliant and insightful when you're writing it but foolish when you look back at it; you know you're moving forward when you're embarrassed by who you were yesterday. It might feel like creating or preserving, but it's all about destroy-ing the unreal, and everything in the dreamstate is unreal, including you. Focused thought is like a laser, so whatever you aim it at will be reduced to ash. Even if you start out trying to defend a belief, you always end up destroying it. Sunlight is the best disinfectant; the best way to get rid of built-up layers of childish belief and emotional debris is to expose it. This is the process of opening your eyes and learning to see. 'You must habit yourself to the dazzle of the light and of every moment of your life,' wrote Whitman. 'Why do my eyes hurt?' asks Neo. 'Because you've never used them before,' answers Morpheus. 'All thought is immoral,' wrote Oscar Wilde. 'It's very essence is destruction. If you think of something, you destroy it. Nothing survives being thought of.' Honest thought leads toward the destruction of the false self and realization of no-self. How could it be otherwise? Do you really think you can haul a lifetime's accumulation of egoic garbage and emotional baggage into any sort of higher spiritual state? This is the real eye of the needle and you can't bring anything with you; everything has to go and this is how it's done. The only way to rid yourself of hardened emotional build-up is through a total purge, and the only way to do that is by reversing the master-slave relationship between heart and mind. You become what you are by *un*becoming what you're not, and the only way I know to do that is the writing process. I'm not married to spiritual autolysis; if you could take a pill or chant a syllable or perform a ceremony and achieve the same result, I'd be talking about that. If meditation worked, I'd be its biggest fan. If someone wakes up by eating ice cream for a year I'll let you know, but until then, you'll have to use your brain.

"Once the process has really started, it takes on a life of its own. It's like going on a physical purification routine and having cleanse reactions; you loosen up all this old stagnated crap in your system and you get sick as these stratified layers of unprocessed waste reenter your bloodstream and reinfect you, but then you purge it out, rest and recover, and start processing the next layer. Go for solo walks to let your thoughts and feelings run free, then return to the writing as you feel the urge. Isolate yourself as much as possible. Get away from the things of man. Live by night to have the world to yourself. Dump pleasures and minimize needs. Don't look ahead, just worry about the next step. You'll know when to walk and ponder, and you'll know when you're ready to pick up the pen and start again. You don't need a list of rules to follow; it's all inside waiting to come out and something much smarter than you or me will support and govern the process. As with a bad case of food poisoning, there's a higher intelligence at work and you're just along for the ride.

"The enemy lurks in shadow. Learn to watch for baseless belief and wishful thinking. Use words precisely, define meanings. Dispense with mystical and foreign terminology; if you can't say it in your mother tongue, it doesn't need saying. Make a study of biases and fallacies so you can see them and eliminate them. Remember that it's not lies you're destroying, it's yourself, and the gentler you are, the more prolonged the process will be. The burning away of untruth leads invariably to no-self. That's where self-inquiry leads, that's where the journey to and through the inner black hole takes you, but knowing where you're going doesn't help just like knowing you have food poisoning doesn't help. You have to go through the purgative process and get the offending toxins out of your system, that's how you go back to the beginning and make a fresh start in the right direction. Compare this focused, high-intensity process to what normally passes for thought and you'll see the real power of your mind when isolated from emotion and ego. By externalizing the process and learning to think lucidly and objectively, you'll see what I mean when I say intelligence is nothing and thinking is everything."

❖

That felt like a heavy answer to a light question, but I get a lot of not-so-good questions so I have to run with the pretty good ones. A few dozen people are sitting on logs, picnic benches, lawn chairs and coolers now. There's a large rock-lined firepit already loaded with logs and brush and ready to be lit, but it's a warm Texas afternoon so fire can wait.

❖

"I've been reading a lot about Taoism lately," says a very large guy in a black t-shirt with a shaved head, wraparound sunglasses and a long beard called Big Greg. He and I spoke earlier. He's a veteran of multiple tours who's seen a lot of action and lost a lot of friends. "They talk about water a lot."

"The highest good resembles water," I say, quoting the *Tao Te Ching*, I think.

"Yeah, how it seeks the path of least resistance, how it can take many forms and overcome obstacles, how the softest thing overcomes the hardest."

I'd like to keep us from descending into tattoo parlor philosophy without being, as has been suggested on occasion, a total jag-off about it. Taoist teachings make for weak philosophy because Taoism is a state of being disguised as an ideology. You can study Taoist thought for the rest of your life and never learn the first thing about Taoism, or you can transition into adulthood and become a Taoist sage instantly because they're just different ways of describing the same state. In theory, Taoism is about adulthood and nothing else. In practice, it's a misguided attempt to convey adulthood to children instead of conveying children to adulthood. If Taoists understood Taoism, they would have been producing a constant stream of adults for the last few millennia, but they haven't so they don't. Like Zen and Advaita, Taoism is all show and no go. It's just another spiritual goosechase resulting in little more than the ego-safe disposal of time and lifeforce.

"Water represents energy," I tell Big Greg and those nearby, "so the comparison between yourself and water can open up your understanding of how your life really works, even in the juvenile state. The water thing is pretty simple. I describe it as pattern, flow and obstruction, and so on. Has your study of Taoism made any significant difference in your life; how you operate, how you understand the world?"

"I don't know, maybe a little," he says.

"I'll take that as a no," I say. "The change we're look-ing for is about as subtle as an earthquake, but that's not what we see because Taoism teaches children how to *act* like adults, not how to *become* adults. Transitioning from childhood to adulthood is not a game of dress-up or make-believe, it's an actual death-rebirth process. As with all solutions offered by the spiritual market-place, Taoism promises the rebirth part without the death part that must come first. That's what keeps the spiritual marketplace in business. They promise you that you can get there from here, but you can't. You have to go all the way back and start over."

"Oh," says Big Greg, looking glum. "I just thought it sounded pretty cool."

"You're right, it *is* pretty cool. If I sat here and told you all the ways my experience of being is different from yours, it would sound so cool you wouldn't believe it; how I live effortlessly and flow through life, how my needs are met and my desires are made manifest, how my internal thoughts and my external environment are interwoven, but what good does my experience do you? You don't need a picture of some better place to hang on your prison wall, you need a map to get you there, and you don't need to worship the map, you need to follow it."

"Oh," he repeats.

"Yeah, okay," he goes on to say.

"The water metaphor is accurate," I continue, "but the point is to become, not act. It's about transition, not growth. It's an actual journey, but you can't make it in a classroom. You're sitting in a dungeon reading a book about life outside the dungeon – Taoism, Nonduality, Zen, the Bible, my books, whatever – but all they really do is pass the time. Your goal should not be to *pass* time but to *seize* it; to use your time and lifeforce to create and expand and discover, not living vicariously through tour guides. You do that by standing up and breaking out of the dungeon, by becoming the hero of your own story and setting out on your own adventure. Then you can throw the books away and write your own. Taoism is fine as far as it goes, but it really doesn't go anywhere. It's not enough to study concepts and try to apply them in your life, you have to make the actual journey, or else you're just relinquishing control and submitting to captivity. That's the wrong kind of surrender you want. The spiritual marketplace promotes surrender in its negative aspect of complacency and inaction, but in its positive aspect, surrender is experienced as yielding and allowing and unifying. You don't make that polar shift through gentle growth but through a cataclysmic transition."

"Sure," says Big Greg, "totally."

"I myself live in alignment with the Tao, but I think of it as pattern. I flow along energetic lines like water; not that I'm *in* the flow but that I have merged *with* it. I don't make hard turns but micro-adjustments so subtle that I'm barely aware of them. I find the path of least resistance naturally, not by controlling but by allowing. I manifest my authentic desires effortlessly because my desires and my dreamstate reality are in harmonious alignment. I have removed my blindfold, dismantled the structure of selfhood, and relaxed into the oceanic currents of being; not *my* being, but being as it manifests around me and through me and *as* me. Correctly understood, this is what Taoism is all about, but it's not a teaching or a practice or a concept, it's a journey of becoming which must begin with a process of *un*becoming. That's the critical step that ego insists we ignore because it entails the dissolution of selfhood itself, and ego will do anything to survive."

"Wow," says Big Greg. "Yeah, okay."

"You're attracted to the spiritual marketplace version of Taoism. That's the negative aspect, but it's the positive aspect you really want. Through no fault of your own, you have committed a serious navigational error and you can never make progress until you go back and correct it. The spiritual marketplace is all about continuing as if no error occurred, and that's why the success rate of awakening – both in and from the dreamstate – is so abysmal. Taoism is just another con game in the spiritual carnival. It has enough bells and whistles to lure you in, and then it dangles some bogus prize for you to play for until your time and lifeforce run out. The spiritual marketplace is not the total failure it appears to be; it's extremely successful in its true objective of holding us prisoner in an unlocked cage and keeping us docile and sedate. By its fruits shall ye know it, and the fruit of the spiritual marketplace is the plodding, cud-munching herd. Think of *Joe versus the Volcano*; Joe Banks sitting in his dungeon-like workplace. No one was making Joe shuffle to his soul-crushing job every day. No one locked him in. He wasn't shackled to his desk. He was free to leave whenever he could muster the resolve, just like you are right now."

"Right," says Big Greg. "Yes."

"Yes," he confirms.

"I'm not picking on you or Taoism," I tell him. "I applaud your discrimination. Zen, Taoism and Advaita are like our children who aren't living up to their potential. They lie to us and steal from us, but we love them anyway because, frankly, they're all we have. Whatever potential they once had has been co-opted and corrupted by ego. Ego doesn't win by force and overcoming, but by the subtle manipulation of fear. Ego wins by avoiding conflict and maintaining the status quo."

"Man," says Big Greg, "okay."

"Sure, totally," he adds upon further reflection.

"The three jewels of Taoism are compassion, moderation and humility, but those aren't pillars of freedom, they're the bars of a cage. Fuck compassion, moderation and humility, and fuck anyone who promotes that bullshit. The watercourse way isn't all about floating down a lazy river. Sometimes it's about battering rapids and pounding waterfalls that tear you to shreds. That's the death that must come before rebirth and there's nothing compassionate, humble or moderate about it."

Big Greg stares at me as if shaken from slumber. I knew from when we met earlier that this guy was a true warrior in a time of false peace. Behind the spiritual fatigue is a man who's had enough of being told to sit quietly and act mellow. He's been repressing his natural instinct to stand up and fight because he's been constantly bombarded with this message of compassion, moderation and humility. He didn't start with Taoism; he's been looking for a cause to follow for a long time, but they've all fallen short. He's mistaken teachings for action and understanding for progress, but he knows a call to action when he hears it. Now, perhaps, he sees that the urge he's been suppressing is the very thing he needs to unleash.

"How hath this weakness taken thee?" I ask him quietly. "Whence springs this inglorious trouble, shameful to the brave? Forbid thyself to feebleness. Be thyself. Wake. Arise. Thus is the soul declared."

He nods.

He smiles.

I sit back for a few minutes while the discussion continues around me. I would take out my phone at this point and do some social networking with my friends, but I don't have a phone or friends or any idea what social networking is. I make a mental note to practice making kissy lips and gangsta peace signs so I can do selfies with my homies should the need arise, but I'm pretty sure it won't. Only recently did I participate – somewhat begrudgingly – in my first high-five, so my socialization proceeds slowly.

A few nearby people have become a little agitated by my insurrectionist views and are expressing support for their cherished -isms, but that's just ego reinforcing its shields. If I push back directly, my energy will be rerouted into those shields and strengthen their emotional resistance. My hope is that if I let people talk enough, eventually they'll hear themselves. I listen to them for a few minutes before deciding I prefer listening to myself.

"Birds naturally fly, fish naturally swim, and humans naturally follow energetic pattern and flow. In a world of adults, there would be no such thing as Taoism because it's really just our own natural development. Everyone would be a novice Taoist sage by their mid-teens. We don't have to teach toddlers the mechanics of standing, walking and running, we just nurture and encourage them and they figure it out on their own. It's the same with the mechanics of adulthood. Being Taoist sages is our stolen birthright; we just have to steal it back."

"So you're a Taoist sage?" asks Big Greg's equally bald, bespectacled and bearded but bigger son, Little Greg.

"I'm not a dues-paying member, but technically, yes, any Human Adult is automatically a Taoist master. Compare Taoism to Balancism. Am I a balance master? Sure, we all are. I'm sure we could all improve a bit, but we've all basically mastered the whole standing and walking thing, right? There's an early lifestage when you're down there on the floor and walking seems magical and mysterious, but you sort it out in the normal course of things and it becomes your natural way of getting around. Once you learn to walk, it doesn't mean your journey is over, it means you're ready to go somewhere. If everyone had their feet strapped together when they were born, then it would be normal for everyone to crawl everywhere and anyone who could stand up and walk would look almost god-like when all they really did was cut their strap and resume their natural development. That's what's going on with us, we were tampered with before we could defend ourselves. We were assimilated into the collective as children. Broken people broke us. Our feet were strapped and we never developed into our natural upright potential. You don't overcome this handicap through compassion, moderation and humility, you do it by cutting the strap and learning to stand and walk on your own. We're not deformed or aberrant or defective, we've just normalized an abnormal condition. If you understood your current condition compared to your natural potential, you wouldn't be compassionate and humble and moderate, you'd be screaming and thrashing in a psychotic rage trying to cut your straps and free yourself from this state of bondage. No price would be too high; you'd cut the strap or cut through your legs without hesitation. The risk of death wouldn't even factor into your thinking. Once you saw that you should be up on your feet, you'd never settle for crawling in the dirt again. So who wants to get this fire started?"

There is applause and hoots of excitement as if we'd all run right out and set Maya's palace ablaze, but I just meant the bonfire.

Goddess IV:
Yield and Overcome

Four days later...

OLD LADY

Okay, where are we?

YIN

We just have a lot of crazy bits and pieces.

OLD LADY

Show me.

LAO TZU

I'm not that happy with it in its current wording.

YANG

You wanna spend the rest of your life in this shack?

LAO TZU

Not really.

YANG

Then *get* happy.

OLD LADY

reads aloud

Ruling the country is like cooking a small fish?

YIN

That's what he said.

LAO TZU

Look, I'm getting really tired.

OLD LADY

You can sleep when you're dead. Right now, write. Why is ruling a country like cooking a small fish? Christ, it sounds like open mic night at a student union. Well?

LAO TZU

I don't know, it just is.

YIN

Look at the rest.

OLD LADY

reads aloud

Use the Tao and evil won't have power to do harm... The sage will be safe... Where are we going with this?

YANG

And what happened to the little fish?

OLD LADY

Yeah, what happened to the little fish? What does a little fish have to do with ruling a country?

LAO TZU

I don't know about the fish, I just said I could go for a little fish and I guess he wrote it down.

YIN

I'm just writing down everything he says. I can't tell the difference between genius and bullshit.

OLD LADY

That's the point, no one can.

YANG

He said some stuff about knowing and not knowing. He can't make up his mind. Knowing is bad, not knowing is good, not knowing you don't know is bad, something like that.

OLD LADY

to Lao Tzu

Why you gotta talk so much shit? Just say the good stuff and you can get outta here.

LAO TZU

I said it's *good* to know what you *don't* know and *bad* to think you know what you *don't* know

YANG

See? He said it again!

OLD LADY

How can we know what we don't know? You have to make sense. You can't just do jazzy stream-of-consciousness stuff. You're writing for soldiers and rice farmers, let's try to keep it simple.

YIN

Listen to this part. When the whole divides into parts the parts need names. There are already too many names.

OLD LADY

Oh c'mon, dude! Whadda ya mean there are too many names? Everything's gotta have a name! You want us to have to go around describing everything all the time because we have too many names?

LAO TZU

I just thought it sounded nice, like, let's not go around giving everything a name all the time. Just let things be what they are. Why be so uptight about labels?

YIN

Because we communicate in symbols, maybe?

YANG

So we can understand each other, maybe?

JED McKenna

LAO TZU

Look, there are like twenty different kinds of pelican, right? Do they all need their own name? An Alsatian Pelican and a Graybeard Pelican and a Speckled Baby-Delivery Pelican... I mean, it's just a freakin' pelican. Lighten up!

OLD LADY

You got a thing against pelicans now?

YANG

So instead of pass the salt, your way I gotta say pass the dried chipmunk skull with the white crystalline substance please?

YIN

The salt can still be what it is, right? Just because we're calling it something doesn't mean it's not salt anymore.

LAO TZU

But it was never really salt in the first place. Salt is just a word, a sound. It's the symbol of a thing, not the thing itself. Let's not mistake symbol for substance, right?

YANG

Wow, wisdom is hard!

LAO TZU

I'm trying to say, uh, don't let the name be the thing, don't let the symbol replace the thingness of the thing. It's not really salt, right? Salt by any other name still tastes just as, uh, salty. I'm just saying we should see things for what they are and not settle for mere labels.

YANG

Why not?

LAO TZU

Because a name is like a finger pointing at the moon, okay? If you focus on the finger, you forget about the moon.

YIN

Oh, that was pretty good. Can I put that in?

OLD LADY

The moon thing? No, but leave the thing about too many names. You can't just give away all the best stuff, you have to make people work for it. How many chapters so far?

YANG

Eighty-one.

OLD LADY

No good. We need a hundred and eight. Very auspicious number.

LAO TZU

I can only do eighty-one. That's an auspicious number too.

OLD LADY

What's so great about eighty-one?

LAO TZU

It's a magic number. Three times three is nine, nine times nine is eighty-one.

OLD LADY

So what? That makes it magic?

LAO TZU

Or, three times three is nine, times three is twenty-seven, times three is eighty-one. Eighty-one is the square of nine and the fourth power of three.

OLD LADY

And *that* makes it magic?

LAO TZU

Eighty-one is the only number, out of *all* numbers, in which the digits add up to its own square root. C'mon, that has to count for something.

OLD LADY

Not really.

LAO TZU

Fine, it's not a magic number, it's just all I can come up with. I tried to get to a hundred and eight but the tank is dry. Seriously, I could cut all this down to half a page.

OLD LADY

Oh *hell* no! We need *more*, not *less*.

LAO TZU

Less *is* more.

OLD LADY

Don't start that crap, we need a book, not a pamphlet. We'll need a preface and a foreword, a bibliography, an epilogue, an index and maybe a concordance to make this thing a book people will pay for. We'll doublespace the whole thing with wide margins and fatten it up with some pretty illustrations; birds and trees and shit.

YIN

Oh, hey! We got one! An illustration! Two fish in a bowl chasing each other in circles!

OLD LADY

Oh yeah? Make it three fish, that's even better.

LAO TZU

Wait! What? No! It has to be *two* fish!

YANG

He's got a real thing about fish.

OLD LADY

Maybe four fish. Four is a very auspicious number.

LAO TZU

No it's not! Four is a stupid number! It doesn't make any sense!

YANG

I think he just says whatever sounds backward and we're supposed to think it's wise.

YIN

reading aloud

If one is sick of sickness, then one is not sick. The perfect square has no corners. A good door needs no lock. Do not tinkle like jade. When the Tao is absent, horses are bred outside the city. One gains by losing and loses by gaining. Knowing others is wisdom, knowing the self is enlightenment.

YANG

Wow! That's really deep!

OLD LADY

Ka-ching!

LAO TZU

He wrote it all down wrong. That's not what I said.

OLD LADY

Who cares what you said? It's not all about *you*. This is the kind of wisdomy shit we're looking for.

LAO TZU

But knowing the self isn't enlightenment because there is no self. It's an illusion!

OLD LADY

Listen Maestro, you gotta get with the program here. You gotta give the people what *they* want, not what *you* want. You start telling people they don't even exist, how're they gonna like that?

LAO TZU

Uh, not much?

OLD LADY

Not much is right! You tell them knowing others is wisdom and knowing themself is enlightenment, they're gonna like that. That's something they can work with. Gives them hope. Got it?

LAO TZU

Yeah, sure, but it's not true.

YANG

You ever wanna get out of here?

LAO TZU

Desperately.

YANG

Then it's true enough.

YIN

True enough, that's good, that's a good thing to aim for.

LAO TZU

But this is my legacy we're talking about! My gift to the world.

OLD LADY

The world's gonna love it. A guy named Venerable Master telling them knowing others is wisdom and knowing themself is enlightenment? Are you kidding me? This stuff is pure gold. We got a bestseller on our hands. Pagodas by the sea for everyone!

LAO TZU

I don't want a pagoda by the sea, I want to go off into the mountains and contemplate, you know, *stuff*.

YIN

So who's stopping you?

LAO TZU

You are! You're holding me prisoner! You're torturing me! All you had to do was see an old man on a water buffalo and wave him through, but you're so bored out here in the middle of nowhere that you decided to treat me like a fly and pull my wings off and make me buzz around in circles!

OLD LADY

Good energy. Let's tap into that.

to Yin

Can we use any of that?

YIN

I don't know. The sage is like a fly with no wings?
He goes nowhere and buzzes around in circles?

YANG

That sounds pretty good.

LAO TZU

It sounds pretty stupid!

OLD LADY

Put a pin in it. Maybe we can spruce it up a bit.
Make it a dragonfly or something.

Total Perspective Vortex

The individual has always had to struggle to keep from being overwhelmed by the tribe. If you try it, you will be lonely often, and sometimes frightened, but no price is too high to pay for the privilege of owning yourself.

Friedrich Nietzsche

"DO YOU CONSIDER YOURSELF TRULY FREE?" asks a smallish, librarianish, sixty-ish woman who looks like she might be taking all this spiritual stuff a little too seriously; more in the everlasting-soul sense than in the hour-upon-the-stage sense. Her smallish, baldish husband is with her, pinching his nose and rubbing his eyes. It starts out as just a casual conversation between them and me, but a crowd gathers as we talk.

"I might think of myself as not *un*free if I thought about it at all," I say, "but I wouldn't say I feel specifically free. I'm in this body on this planet and that comes with certain restrictions, but I don't have any sense of being *un*free so it's not really an issue."

She just stares at me.

"If you're uncomfortable due to the constraints of your egoic structure," I continue, "then you have two solutions; get free or get comfortable. I advocate the former and the spiritual marketplace promotes the latter."

"But now you're free, right?" she presses. I detect a degree of selective deafness.

"Once upon a time I felt so painfully constrained that I was consumed by a burning mania to get free or die trying. I didn't attain real freedom, of course, I just broke out of my juvenile structure, and that allowed the natural unfolding of my spiritual DNA. That's all anyone can do; escape from their egoic restraints and expand into their transpersonal, transegoic potential. That's awake *in* the dreamstate. There's also awake *from* the dreamstate – enlightenment – but that's more like freedom from appearance, consciousness without an object, which probably isn't what you're asking about."

She stares blankly at me. My answer does nothing for her, but I didn't think it would. The three states of consciousness are awake *from* the dreamstate, awake *in* the dreamstate, and *asleep* in the dreamstate. She seems to think there's another one called freedom, or maybe she's referring to adulthood which may look like freedom through a child's eyes. If adulthood is what she's after, I'll have to disappoint her. There are exceptions, but the belated transition to adulthood most often occurs between twenty-six to thirty-four, so what I'm really telling her is that she missed the boat twice and there won't be a third. Breaking out of the herd and resuming one's normal course of development is a young person's game, and this woman is not young.

❖

I inhabit the spacetime, energymatter, causalistic, dualistic dreamstate, but this isn't my paradigm-of-residence any more than it's yours. The dreamstate is an artificial reality, so it's obviously no one's home. We identify with our body, our place in space and time, our country and our planet, our family and our society and, of course, our ego-self, but all that is just appearance, and that thou aren't. This is where revisiting your assumptions can make a real difference.

Our brightest minds aren't always our best thinkers, which is good news for people of modest intellect such as myself because it means we're not excluded from this ultimate game. It's not a great intellect that's required, but a functional intellect uncorrupted by fear-based emotion. Erasmus estimated our emotion-to-reason ratio at 24:1 which seems right. Mind is the dreamstate killer, but it can't do much harm when swaddled in layers of emotional insulation. To have any hope of awakening in or from the dreamstate, we must minimize the negative impact of emotion and maximize the power of thought through the process of spiritual autolysis, not merely in the sense of writing, but in the sense of going to war with pen for sword and yourself as enemy.

The power of thought is your secret weapon – *pashupatastra!* – and you've had it all along, but thinking doesn't work the way you think it does. It can't be done in your heart-controlled head, and that's why I am now offering, for a limited time only, Sri Sri Sri Sri Jed's Spiritual Autolysis Super Seminar. For less than the cost of a few new cars, you can attend a weekend workshop with me in which I'll teach you about this groundbreaking process and how it can guide you into the fun and exciting world of spiritual enlightenment. Or, for the budget-minded seeker, we offer the entire course on DVD for less than the price of a Caribbean cruise for six. Actually, all you need is a pen, some paper, and a desire to get real. Keep doing spiritual stuff if you think it's working for you, but remember, you already have the power to awaken both in and from the dreamstate, so the only question is, do you want to be one of the first fifty to sign up and receive a free Tibetan singing bowl? Operators are standing by.

◈

I share a story about former galactic president Zaphod Beeblebrox, which the librarian does not seem to appreciate. Zaphod was sentenced to enter a contraption called the Total Perspective Vortex; a small torture chamber in which one was, for a brief instant, forced to confront their complete and total insignificance by seeing the immensity of time and space with themselves represented by a tiny dot in the middle labeled, "You are here." The direct awareness of one's meaninglessness was so devastating that everyone who entered the Total Perspective Vortex fell out, not just dead but soul-crushed. Delightfully egotistic and egoistic Zaphod, however, survived. He interpreted this not as a revelation of his total nothingness, but as confirmation that he was, as he'd always assumed, the center of the universe. And he was correct. The infinite universe is just a belief. Your awareness is your only direct experience of reality and, like Zaphod, you would be correct in considering yourself to be the center of your own private universe.

> Everything you see or hear or experience in any way at all is specific to you. You create a universe by perceiving it, so everything in the universe you perceive is specific to you.   -Douglas Adams

The real reason Zaphod survived, as I recall, is that he was in a simulation when he entered the Total Perspective Vortex, and that shielded him from the usual outcome. He didn't know he was in an artificial reality at the time, but I always do, so if you stuck me in there, what you'd hear from me would not be a blood-curdling wail of mind-shredding agony, but a request for a large popcorn and a fizzy drink.

◈

"What do you mean by spiritual DNA?" asks the librarian lady, whose name, I learn, is Ellie.

"We are unique crystalline snowflakes in an endless blizzard of unique crystalline snowflakes," I say, ignoring her theatric eye roll. Fifteen or twenty people are listening in now so I'm trying to make this of general interest. "We shine the light of our lifeforce through our unique crystalline pattern into the dreamstate theater, and we inhabit the reality we project."

"Meaning," she continues, "that we're prisoners of what you call our spiritual DNA? We can never be free?"

She's like a dog digging for a bone she'll never find because she only dreamed it in the first place. She won't awaken in or from the dreamstate, but like anyone, she might have a more pleasant experience of it if she were hauling less baggage. Happiness increases with the slicing away of false beliefs, but Ellie seems not only attached to her burden, but eager to increase it.

There is a fruitbearing apple tree nearby. I summon it to my aid.

"Behold yon apple tree," I say. "What freedom does it have? It expresses its own unique pattern without volition. How free or unfree does it feel? What choice does it have in anything? An appleseed can't choose to become a daisy or a pony; does that make it unfree? It has a built-in pattern it must follow or it will fail to germinate and never discover its potential. Where in nature does freedom exist?"

I continue before she can bang the gong of freedom again.

"Behold me. I am awake both in and from the dreamstate – both adult and enlightened – but what freedom do I have? Several decades ago I experienced an explosive event that sent me hurtling off in a single, specific direction. That direction of travel is not what I *do*, it's what I *am*, but it's still just a role I play. I'm just going along for the ride, enjoying the show and play-ing my part. What other freedom can there be but the freedom to express your authentic nature? To discover your nature *by* expressing it? The closest thing to the freedom you seek is found through the severing of attachments, including the attachment to freedom."

❖

No real freedom is possible because there's no real self to be free, but what about the *appearance* of freedom? The faux-freedom of the faux-self? Is that possible? Sure, why not? What can't be dreamt? Paint your prison cell with green fields and blue skies and puffy white clouds and pretend you're a bird. Or paint it with ghosts or aliens or higher-order beings, or angels and demons, or the psychedelic vomit of your subconscious, whatever your egoic structure calls for. That's what Ellie keeps calling for. She doesn't want freedom, she wants a spiritual makeover. She doesn't want to escape captivity, she wants to be happier within it. That's why she finds my answers unsatisfying; they don't fit her question. I don't have all answers to all questions, I only have one answer and it's your job to arrive at the right question. Spiritual teachers are doing their students a disservice by validating invalid questions when they should be swatting their students mercilessly with sticks, but then they'd lose their students and couldn't play teacher anymore. If you were sitting across from me right now and you started blubbering about your feelings or experiences or hopes and dreams, about freedom or love or bliss or compassion or whatever visions of sugarplums dance in your head, instead of hitting you with a stick, I'd give you a jolt with my *Wakey-Wakey Taser* to snap you out of it, or maybe I'd use the longer *Satori Now! Cattle Prod* so I didn't have to reach so far. *Zap!* Right on the third eye. *Shocktipat!* I bet that would leave a mark.*

---

* *Wakey-Wakey Taser, Satori Now! Cattle Prod, and Shocktipat!* are the intellectual property of Sri Sri Sri Sri Jed Enterprises, a subsidiary of The Inland Sea Whaling Company. "Namaste: We bow to the consumer within you."

"So you're saying there's no such thing as freedom?" Ellie presses, her tone suggesting that failure to reinforce her illusion of freedom would reflect poorly on me as a spiritual solution-provider, perhaps even earning me a downward-facing thumb mudra.

"Freedom exists in context. If you were caught in a bear trap, the freedom-urge would be so powerful that you'd chew off your leg to achieve it. In spiritual terms the question is, what do you want to be free from so desperately that you'd chew off your own head?"

"So we're not free to choose what we'll become?" she insists. "We're not really free at all."

"Like yon apple tree, there's no need to decide what you'll become, only to allow the natural unfolding of what you are. Expressing your unique pattern, your spiritual DNA, is your natural source of happiness, anything else is just compensating for being out of alignment with your nature. That misalignment is really the only thing to be free from. No one is born to the herd. It's not in anyone's authentic nature to be a productive member of society and go to church once a week and Disneyville once a year. That's halfborn, herdbound pattern, not fullborn, individual pattern."

"You still haven't answered her question," says the librarian's accountant-ish husband who looks like he's comfortably settled into the herd and unlikely to be making any life choices bigger than Accord versus

Camry. (I would later learn that the librarian was a chemist and the accountant was a labor negotiator.)

"The answer is to use the spiritual autolysis process to explore your desire for freedom; figure out what it really is and how to get rid of it. Freedom is just a buzzword. It's not a goal, it's an obstruction, so you have to dislodge it to restore free flow. You need freedom from your attachment to freedom. That's where you're stuck, and you can use the writing process to get unstuck."

I'm eager to dislodge this freedom topic and restore some flow to this conversation.

"Imagine you're a spaceman in your spacesuit working outside your spaceship," I say, ignoring her pained expression and gutteral moan. "One minute your dramatic context is representing your family, country and humanity in space, playing many roles to many audiences in a full, rich, complex life, and the next minute your tether snaps and you go floating off into the void with no hope of rescue. Just like that, all context is gone and you're completely on your own. You've died out of your life, but you're still alive. You're free now, but you can't exert any control over your situation. Your trajectory is determined from the outset, so unless you get hit by a satellite or bump into a comet, that's your speed and heading for the rest of your life."

"And what's the point of this hypothetical scenario?" asks Ellie impatiently.

"The point is that it's not hypothetical, it's where you are right now. You're still tethered to the mothership which provides the illusion of context and meaning, but free-floating in black, empty space is where you really are. It's not until your emotional tether snaps that you awaken to the reality of your situation. So that's where we are in this metaphor; your tether has snapped and you're floating off into the void. What's next?"

I wait a few beats before answering my own question for the entire group.

"What's next is the Total Perspective Vortex; the shrieking madness of the relative mind confronting absolute truth. Self confronts no-self. Finite brain confronts infinite mind. That's enlightenment; awareness without appearance, consciousness without an object. A little of that kind of freedom goes a long way. Within moments, you've had enough freedom and you want your dreamstate back. You want lies and drama and pain to give you purpose and meaning. You want context even if it's false. You want other people to love and hate. You want your beloved beliefs and opinions to give you shape and definition. You want the pain of a toothache and the boredom of standing in line. You want goals to achieve and battles to win, even if it's just a pointless game. You want to slip back into the only character you've always played, even if it was never really you. You want to feel hope and connection, and you don't care if it's a lie because nothing is worse than nothing. A dreamless sleep is one thing, but a waking dreamlessness is totally something else. Anything that distracts from the mind-ravaging horror of Nothing Forever is good, even delusion and ego. Any context is better than no context. Freedom is the real prison and the dreamstate is the only escape. Maya's not *keeping* us from truth, she's *saving* us from it. Nothing Forever is the nightmare scenario, not just for us but for consciousness itself. Brahman needs Maya, but Maya doesn't exist so Brahman has to dream her into being. In the same way that we're stuck in small cells and decorate them to keep ourselves amused, Brahman is stuck in the infinitely empty cell of Nothing Forever, and creation is the paint job that keeps Brahman amused. Infinite consciousness creates a faux reality from which it can't escape because there's nothing out there; the dreamstate *is* the escape. The false-finite is the solution to the problem of the true infinite. Maya and the dreamstate and even the ego-self aren't some terrible enemy to be overcome, they are salvation itself. Of course it's all bullshit; it *has* to be. Maya is protecting us from the *real* reality of Nothing Forever. She's not a goddess, she's God, and the dreamstate universe you inhabit is her creation. That's what's really going on here. Pretty trippy, right?"

I nod vigorously in agreement with myself. I expect the assembled group to instantly achieve abiding non-dual awareness, but what I get instead is Ellie asking, "So you're saying freedom is bad?" I'd like to encourage her to revisit her clearly ironic attachment to freedom, but her dogged persistence is wearing me down.

"The freedom-urge is good in the context of motivating change, but it isn't the dreamstate that you want to be free from, it's the prison of your own egoic shell. Like everyone, you're stuck at a developmental age between ten and twelve; that's what you want to be free of. Arrested development is the only spiritual issue anyone needs to address."

I can see she's about to ask about freedom again, so I rush ahead before she gets the chance.

"The purpose of the dreamstate is to create the appearance of false-something despite the reality of true-nothing. The dreamstate is a refuge from truth where awareness can experience drama and conflict and spectacle as an antidote to boredom. That's why waking *from* the dreamstate is the booby-prize; you're effectively tunneling *out* of a cosmic playground and *into* the prison of Nothing Forever. Mind is the dreamstate killer, but do you really want to kill the dreamstate? Where would you be without it? We think Maya and ego and emotional attachment are the enemy because they separate us from the holy grail of truth, but it's really the other way around; we're not in the dreamstate to *find* truth, we're here to get *away* from it. Maya's Palace of Illusion is a prison from one perspective and salvation from another, and Maya herself, despite not existing, is both jailer and liberator, demon and angel. That's why adulthood is better than enlightenment, why false-relative is better than true-absolute, why containment is better than freedom. The dreamstate isn't the problem and truth isn't the solution, it's the other way around."

"Okay, fine," says Ellie tersely. "I understand exactly what you're saying, but what about freedom?"

Medifuckintation

All the powers in the universe are already ours.
It is we who have put our hands before our eyes
and cry that it is dark.

Swami Vivekananda

I ALWAYS GET A LITTLE PUSHBACK about my views on meditation, but I don't concern myself with resistance. The only way this attempt at communication between us can work is if the effort comes from both directions. I do my part and anyone who does their part to meet me halfway across the invisible divide stands some chance of receiving and processing the ideas I'm expressing; then they can make their own decisions and, perhaps, their own crossing.

Many of these ideas seem totally crazy to me when I view them from the perspective of the chronically herdbound — no belief is true, reality's not real, no-self is true self, Rocky and Bullwinkle were lovers — but they're not meant to be accepted or believed, they're simply breadcrumbs and coming attraction reels; postcards from beyond the edge. Until you see it for yourself, it all sounds totally crazy. I used to see everything the way everyone does, of course, but now it's as if I'm looking at people from a distance and instead of countless individuals, I see one person with an endless variety of masks. This person is both masculine and feminine, victim and villain, creator and destroyer. From this elevation I see love in its negative aspect of fearful grasping and in its positive aspect of joyous release. I can zoom out and lose sight of humanity entirely, or I can zoom in and see your face.

Totally crazy.

Awakening is a paradigm-level event, meaning that it's all-inclusive. It's not like taking up cribbage or learning to weave, it's like dying from one kind of being and being reborn as a completely different kind of being. There's no way I can amp up my transmission to reach someone who resists it and there's no reason to try. Apple trees don't force their fruit on anyone or promote the nutritional merits of the apple or set up roadside fruit stands. They make their fruit and let it fall where it may. They act, but don't reflect on the fruit of the act.

I never lose sight of the fact that nothing is wrong and that nothing needs to be fixed. Suffering is just a single melodic theme in the tragicomic symphony of any given life; an air on the string of I. If delusion feels like a dungeon to you, then you have two choices; make yourself more comfortable in the dungeon or get out of it. I awoke in and from the dreamstate in response to a terrible psycho-spiritual pain; not by fleeing from it but by going into it, and whatever else that pain may have been, it was honest.

◇

"Some spiritual teachings advocate meditating for fifteen or twenty minutes once or twice a day," I tell the assembled group of thirty and growing. "Just a little something you can squeeze in before breakfast or after dinner like a power-walk or a plankton-enriched bitterroot smoothie; a little squirt of lubricant to scratch a spiritual itch without making it bleed. If all you want is an increase in mental clarity, meditation is great – I do something similar myself – but it certainly has nothing to do with awakening in or from the dreamstate. Just the opposite, in fact. The real point of silencing the mind is silencing the mind. No one who finds a few minutes for meditation in their busy schedule could ever be more than a spiritual dilettante with less hope of waking in or from the dreamstate than if they did nothing at all. The real issue they're addressing is not that they're asleep, but that they're not asleep enough.

"A serious approach to meditation would be more like the inverse, where you get a fifteen-minute break from meditation twice a day to grab a bite and hit the head. No job, no family, no holidays, no other agenda or priority; all day, every day, do-or-die. Sell the house, sell the car, sell the kids, or give them away, or just abandon them, who cares? You watch your sanity go, your health go, anything you ever called a life go. Of course, you'll probably die in the process – those are the stakes at this level of gameplay – but if you think meditation is the path to something you want, then stop dabbling and commit yourself. Go to your mountain retreat, live on power bars and water, and meditate your ass off. Will it work? On the face of it I can't see why it would, but when mind and heart are focused, what's not possible? What can't you dream? Of course, no one is really going to meditate for twenty-three and a half hours every day, and there's no reason they should. I've presented a technique that can't fail to result in awakening, so why seek on a remote mountaintop what you can find at your kitchen table?

"The cocreative process is active in all of us and works whether we're aware of it or not. If you tell the universe in the way the universe understands that you would rather die than continue living a lie, then the universe will understand and your desire will unfold, not through magic but through energetic alignment.

If, on the other hand, your desire to awaken is about as powerful as your desire to watch a ballgame or eat a sandwich, then you'll get what you play for. The dreamstate universe is mind and Brahman is mind and you are mind – there's no true distinction – so processes like manifestation and cocreation are no different from convection or condensation; when the cause is right, the effect occurs.

"Some people are more attuned to this cocreative dynamic and most are less, but it works for everyone to whatever degree they're able to eliminate ego from the equation and allow the process to unfold. This is the functional reality of the dreamstate; finite and infinite mind are reunited when the segregating barrier of ego is removed and integration is thus restored. Integration of self and environment is not based on belief or faith or merit, it's based on the simple mechanics of adulthood. If the pieces are in place, the machine works. You are not *in* the universe, you *are* the universe. Not someone else's universe in which you're just a background element, but your *own* universe in which you are Player One. As you become more lucid, the distinction between player and program dissolves and you become a participant in the creation and shaping of your gamespace reality.

"Is meditation a way to awakening? Not a direct one, but I guess it could be. So could removing your flesh one ounce per day or applying hot rocks to your chakras or smoking a shitload of dope. The main thing is not the act itself, but the intent and desire that inform the act. Meditate for half an hour a day and you'll get some trivial benefits unrelated to spiritual advancement. Meditate for all *but* half an hour a day and you can't *fail* to awaken, not because meditation leads to awakening but because it's your dreamstate and it's responsive to your authentic desires. You tell it what you want through action and focused intent, and your reality reshapes itself to your will and desire. Your wish is your dreamstate's command."

◈

"A teacher of awakening who was fully committed to the complete and total success of each and every student would be an unthinkable monster. No one would stay in the same room with such a person for more than two minutes, but anyone who did would end up transitioning into the integrated state and would forever honor and cherish the monster who got them there. When you picture the perfect guru, don't imagine silken-haired, blue-eyed Jesus carrying a baby lamb or Samuel Graynamore fanning out no-limit credit cards, imagine O'Brien torturing Winston Smith, again and again and again.

"The dreamstate is a tragicomic dramatic production. It's not all tragedy or all comedy; it's both. To the degree that it's a comedy, it's a dark one because no one lives happily ever after. To the degree that it's a tragedy, it's a light one because no one lives *un*happily ever after. Everyone dies and rots and gets eaten by worms or goes up in smoke. When the game is over, kings and pawns go back in the same box. I'm aware that all of you fell into the traps and snares of the spiritual marketplace and are stuck in them even now, but you are within range of this message and you're trying to be receptive to it, so the potential is there. Maybe someone among you will let these ideas pierce their chest plate and say yes, they will make a break from herdmind or die trying. Then, whatever you do – whether it's spiritual autolysis or meditating yourself beyond madness or standing on one leg for the rest of your life – your universe will understand what you want and it will reshape your dreamstate to make it happen because that's how this whole cocreative thing really works. Ultimately, it's not really a cocreative process at all because there's no duality; dreamer and dream are one, Brahman and Maya are one, you and your dreamstate environment are one. As soon as you learn to reshape your reality, you can use it to build cities or lead armies or create great art as many have before you, or you can use it to open your eyes and express your unique spiritual DNA and go where no one has gone before. That doesn't happen in twenty minutes a day or because you burn incense and wear organic cotton and have a coexist bumper sticker on your car, or because you chant or pray or read the words of great masters, or because your chakras are tuned and your aura is vivid, it happens when you tell the universe in the way the universe understands that there will be no other thought or priority or secondary objective until you wake up or die trying. That's what spiritual success looks like, and that's why billions of seekers, far more intelligent and dedicated and courageous than myself, never had a chance.

"You are not a person with an abyss inside, you are the abyss itself, and what you consider self is just the emotional clutter and debris that conceals the truth of your inner black hole. The abyss of infinite, featureless awareness is the truth of no-self, and the clutter and debris is the lie of ego-self. Spiritual progress isn't the feel-good, sweetness-and-light honeytrap we're so eager to fall into, it's mathematical and certain and precise and follows strict and immutable laws. There is not the least bit of wiggle room, no skipping of steps or bending of rules, no deus ex machina or mystical intervention. No one can ever know who and what and where they really are until they become it."

❖

"Who of us truly believes there's anything beyond the black hole? Who of us believes that when the self is deconstructed, there's anything left? Who believes that when you step into the void, your death is followed by a rebirth and that a new and different kind of life awaits? I'm not asking who thinks it sounds good or who wishes it were true, but who is so sure it's true that if I took you to the lip of the volcano, you'd willingly step in. Raise your hand if your belief is that strong."

There's some indecision but no hands go up.

"Of course not, the universal answer is no. No one's belief is that strong. How could it be? It's not a short-coming in you, it's not a personal failing, it's the same for everyone. It was the same for me. In my two-year journey to the volcano it never even occurred to me that I might survive the process. No one really thinks there's anything beyond the inner abyss, beyond the end of self. No one really thinks they can survive the step into the volcano. No one really believes there's anything beyond the seen and known of the material world, but some take that step anyway. Why? Because it's not a leap of faith, it's a leap of surrender, a trust-fall into the void. Nobody takes this step from egoic vanity or spiritual desire or religious longing, you only take it because your eyes are open and you see that an honest death is better than a dishonest life. You see that you have nothing to lose. I can tell you what's on the other side of the gateless gate and I can describe it in a hundred books, but you'll never believe it until you pass through and see it for yourself. This is true of everyone, no exceptions. No one truly believes there's anything beyond. If we really believed we'd become enlightened by jumping into a magic volcano, then we'd all flock in like lemmings, but that's not how it works. It's not about strength of belief and it never was. It's not a leap of faith, it's a leap of hyper-lucidity

167

and radical sanity. Sorry, I know that's a drag, but it's better to know the truth than to go on thinking that your problem is that you don't have enough faith or belief, or that you're not genetically or culturally pre-disposed toward awakening, or that you just haven't found the right teacher or teaching yet. That's not the issue. No one jumps out of a burning skyscraper as long as not jumping is still an option. There are no early adopters in that situation. You never take the next step until the ground crumbles beneath your feet. If you're not on your way to and through that inner black hole, it's because your hatred for your false-self is not burning bright enough, which means you're not clearly perceiving the artificial nature of this reality and your character, which means your eyes are closed. If you want to open your eyes, you have to think more honestly and aggressively than you think possible. Use spiritual autolysis to think better, to awaken the Little Bastard within, to open your eyes and see what is instead of keeping them closed and seeing what's not. Then, slipping into that black hole becomes as easy as slipping into a warm bath. Or maybe you die. Either way, problem solved."

Goddess V:
The Eternal Tao

YIN

I'm not sure this guy really is a wise man. I think maybe he just said that to complete the form. He's probably a spy or a secret agent or something.

YANG

to Lao Tzu

How 'bout it? Are you really a wise man?

LAO TZU

Well, there are no specific guidelines, but pretty much, yeah.

YANG

Quick, say something wise!

LAO TZU

Returning is the motion of the Tao.

OLD LADY

Oh, *snap!* I just got chills. I'm already thinking sequel: *Tao Te Dieux: The Force Awakens.*

YIN

Is that true? The returning motion thing?

YANG

Who cares if it's true, it *sounds* true.

OLD LADY

Yeah, write that down the way he said it. Don't let him change it later.

YANG

What does it mean?

OLD LADY

Who cares what it means? It means whatever people think it means. We just have to worry about how it sounds and that sounds freakin' awesome!

YIN

to Lao Tzu

You keep sayin' stuff like that and we'll have you outta here in no time.

LAO TZU

Yeah? Like four days ago?

YANG

Don't be cranky, you're doing good work. You're helping the people of China and the world. You'll be remembered forever.

LAO TZU

For what? Selling out? Repackaging truth for public consumption? Turning wisdom into a cheap commodity? Poisoning the minds of the people with sugar when they crave sustenance?

YANG

Uh, yeah, I guess.

YIN

You should be happy. What are the odds that a couple of nice border guards and an old laundry lady would stop you and turn your garbled ramblings into a sacred text?

YANG

Yeah, don't be all high and mighty. If we had just waved you through no one would have ever heard of you. Now you'll be famous forever!

OLD LADY

You did good with that returning motion thing. Say more stuff like that.

LAO TZU

Okay, here you go. Why are the people starving? Because the rulers eat up the money in taxes. Why are the people rebellious? Because the rulers interfere too much. Why do the people think so little of death? Because the rulers demand too much of life.

OLD LADY

Oy vey!

YANG

Make him stop!

YIN

Jesus Christ! I can't write that down!

LAO TZU

Why not? It's true enough. Isn't that what you're looking for, true enough?

YIN

You think you can say crazy shit because you're leaving the country, but they'll have our heads if I write that.

OLD LADY

Try to be a little more upbeat. Happy wisdom, not crazy wisdom.

LAO TZU

The humble is the root of the noble. The low is the foundation of the high.

OLD LADY

Yeah, that's better. Is it true?

LAO TZU

I don't know. It was in a fortune cookie I got in a Chinese restaurant once.

YIN

You don't have to say Chinese.

YANG

Yeah, it's assumed.

OLD LADY

Holy shit! Is that what's going on here?

she rifles through parchments, stopping to read from different parts

Let's see here, yep, yep. Gibberish, gibberish, fortune cookie. Gibberish, gibberish, fortune cookie. It's all gibberish and fortune cookies! This guy's just been stringing us along this whole time.

YANG

Let's beat his ass!

OLD LADY

No, wait! Fortune cookie and gibberish might be a recipe for a bestseller, right? He's obviously holding back the good stuff so he can write his own book later. We just squeeze the best stuff out of him, make it all kind of blurry and vague, add a lot of cheap filler to thicken it up, and we'll have our book! It's a lot easier to *sound* wise than to *be* wise!

LAO TZU

Those who know when they have enough are rich. There is no greater misfortune than greed. Full of desire you see the manifestation, free from desire you see the mystery.

OLD LADY

There! See? Fortune cookie wisdom!

YIN

Yeah, but how many ways can you say the same few things? How much can we really stretch it out?

YANG

Good point. Without the gibberish we only have a few pages. The more gibberish the better! Hey Maestro, say some more gibberish.

LAO TZU

The sage is guided by what he feels and not by what he sees. He lets go of that and chooses this.

OLD LADY

Write it!

YIN

Got it!

LAO TZU

C'mon people, this is exactly what I'm talking about, this difference between the authentic and the artificial. The way you guys are going, you'll give rise to generations of Taoists who *act* sagely instead of becoming sages. You're going to send people looking in the wrong direction.

Yin, Yang and Old Lady huddle for a quiet discussion before resuming their positions.

YIN

to Lao Tzu

Okay, you can go.

LAO TZU

Go? Go where? What? Why?

YANG

Leave. Get your Bubby out of the impound lot and go. That's what you want, right? Leave China? So fine, leave! You go now. So long. Bye-bye!

OLD LADY

We don't need you, Maestro. We can make a better book without you. All your truth is just messing things up. People don't want that shit. You would sell like ten books, friends and family, local library, that's it! Who cares? We fix it up and sell like a gazillion books! People will buy our book for a thousand years.

LAO TZU

But it's just garbage! You're betraying your audience!

OLD LADY

At least we'll *have* an audience! Your way, no audience. Catch twenty-two. Be honest and unpopular or dishonest and popular. At least our way, maybe a little truth gets out to the people. Your way, it ends here and you die unknown.

YIN

No one's telling you not to be honest, we just don't want you messing up our book.

YANG

We got the recipe now; four parts gibberish to one part fortune cookie. We don't need your help.

LAO TZU

Help? It's *my* book! I *am* the Venerable Master! What are *you?* A coupla border guards and a cleaning lady. Who are you people to write the *Tao Te Ching?*

OLD LADY

Bad title. We need something with more pizzazz.

YIN

The Wonderful Way of the Way?

YANG

Truth, Justice and the Chinese Way?

OLD LADY

No, we need sex appeal. *The Tao of the Large-Breasted Goddess with the Shapely Behind*, something like that.

YANG

Wow! I'd buy that book and I don't even know how to read!

YIN

You have to give the people what they want.

LAO TZU

No, you have to give them the *truth*, even if they *don't* want it.

OLD LADY

Seriously, do you ever listen to yourself?

LAO TZU

Okay, that's it! I'm not going anywhere. I can't stop you from ruining this project with your complete lack of insight and your corruption and your greed, but I can at least try to get a few good points in. I'll help you write your dumb book, but you have to let me have some say in it, okay?

OLD LADY

Yeah, yeah. Okay Maestro. Look, maybe you got some wisdom, I don't know. I'm a simple person. I wake up, I do a bunch of stuff, I go to sleep, nothing fancy. Maybe you're fancy with a lot of wisdom and stuff, nice for you. To me, you look pretty regular, like you wake up, do a bunch of stuff and go to sleep. Where's the wisdom part? I don't know. You say you're wise, fine, you're wise. What do I know?

LAO TZU

The sage knows without traveling. He sees without looking. He accomplishes much without doing anything.

OLD LADY

Yeah, sure. Nice work if you can get it. You say some good stuff, but is it true? I don't know. How do I apply it in my own life? I don't. I'm just an old lady. Maybe if I was young again I'd be excited and do a lot of Tao stuff and become a wise old lady riding around on water buffaloes and saying clever shit all day, but I'm just a simple person.

LAO TZU

See simplicity in the complicated. Achieve greatness in little things.

OLD LADY

Write it.

YIN

Got it.

OLD LADY

That's what I mean. I'm in the rice paddy for ten hours a day, I do laundry, raise kids, care for the elderly, cook, clean, and try to maintain order, and now you come along and say achieve greatness in little things, and I ask myself, is this guy some great prophet lighting the way to heaven, or just some goofball riding a water buffalo talking like a fortune cookie?

LAO TZU

The truth probably lies somewhere in-between.

OLD LADY

Speaking of which, I just heard from my cousin Jimmy over in India. They got a guy now – the Boobie, the Booty, something like that – they say he talks about a middle way...

There's a knock at the door.

YANG

Jesus, seriously? Fourteen years and not a soul, now it's standing room only.

YIN

Who's there?

LAO TZU

It's her. Open the door. Don't make her wait.

OLD LADY

Her who?

LAO TZU

The one you just summoned. The Large-Breasted Goddess with the Shapely Behind.

OLD LADY

I just made that shit up!

LAO TZU

Maybe you did. We don't know how things work when gods are involved.

Yang opens the door revealing Bubby.

YANG

There's no one here but the old man's water buffalo.

LAO TZU

Bubby!

BUBBY

May I come in?

YANG

Holy shit! The fuckin' thing talks!

BUBBY

Is that a yes? Let's call that a yes.

Bubby enters.

Marichelle 9:
Broken Compass

Maybe you think I'm crazy because I say crazy things. I don't mind if I'm crazy but don't be too sure. Don't give up so quick. There's more to see.

*

Try not to be too in love with all your conclusions. Let go of the conclusions you have and see what other ones come in. Don't hold onto them so hard. They're all wrong anyway so maybe that makes it easier to let go.

*

Being done with old conclusions is a big part of this, even more than having new conclusions, I would say. I don't know if I have any conclusions really. I can't think of any right now.

*

Don't worry so much about the outside world and all the people and nature and everything. That doesn't matter. Worry about inside instead. Everything makes pretty good sense when you see it right, or maybe stop seeing it wrong.

*

Waking up out of coma is not something people want to know about. If they wanted to know, they'd already know because it's really the most obvious thing. There are no secrets about anything, there's only where you look and where you don't look.

*

We think there's all kinds of mystery and secrets, but I would say there's not. Everything is very obvious if you look. Why it's a mystery is the real mystery. Why don't we look? That's the really crazy thing.

*

This is like the easiest level. It's so obvious that you have to ask why you didn't know this your whole life. This isn't top secret or high level or anything, it's just very basic.

*

Why they didn't tell you this in school is a good question. The answer is they didn't know, okay? Nobody told them so they didn't tell you. That's not so bad, it's just how it works. If you want to do something different that's up to you.

*

Take a look at this word spiritual. Maybe it's not as good as you think. Maybe it confuses things more than it clears them up, okay? Maybe that's a good place to start looking.

*

You can say everything is spiritual or nothing is, but you can't say some things are spiritual and some things aren't, like good stuff is spiritual and bad stuff is something else. You can't cut it up that way. Spiritual doesn't mean nice, it means everything.

*

The word spiritual is like a broken compass that sends you the wrong way because you think it works okay. Maybe that's what you really want, to go the wrong way and never get where you're going. Maybe you like your compass to be broken, I don't know.

*

Things are not always clear in this area. It's hard to tell what you want when you don't even know. It might be good to figure out what you want before you go looking for it, but we don't always make total sense.

*

Spiritual doesn't mean anything. It's a wrong word. It's based on wrong ideas about things. If you like your wrong ideas about everything that's fine, but if you want to come out of coma you have to say goodbye to wrong ideas. That's a good conclusion you can let go of.

*

The only thing you can do is get out of coma. Anything else is inside coma which just means more of this crazy world. How much reality do you think there is if you're still in the coma? Pretty much zero, I would say.

*

Don't worry about leaving, there's no place else to go. Coma is where we live, but you can go see what's out there. You can go out and have a nice look around, but then you always come back, no big deal.

*

People are easy to fool, that's their main feature. Once you have this feature there can be anything, right? Being easy to fool is the most important thing because then there can be anything and it's all just as real as anything else.

*

You're sure that you're a human, right? You think there's so much evidence that it must be true and everyone agrees, but without proof there's just evidence. Evidence is for belief and proof is for knowing, okay? Human is just a kind of monkey, I would say.

*

I don't have to make sense anymore. I made sense for a long time and that was enough. You can only make so much sense before it's too much. I am very comfortable with this level of sense. It's like the temperature thing on the wall. This is right where I like it.

*

There is no real value of anything. Nothing has real value of its own. Something has value because you say it has value. There is only the value you believe. The real value of everything is nothing. That's a good thing to know.

✳

If you think coma is real, you're crazy, but if every-one is crazy then maybe it's not so crazy. Then maybe I'm the crazy one and you should be explaining things to me.

✳

To you everything is pretty obvious, but this isn't about obvious, it's about what you can be sure about, which is a lot less than you think. You should go back and take a closer look. I would say that's the main thing you could do.

✳

The answer is that you're insane, so that must be what you came here to ask. That's what you want to know even if you don't know it. Are you insane? Yes, you are very insane. I hope that helps.

✳

Be careful of people who tell you you're not insane and you're not in coma and everything is just fine. That's what you like to hear but it's not true, it just makes you feel better. If you just want to feel better you should get a massage or have an extra dessert or something.

Belated Rebirth Matrices

The psyche of the individual is commensurate
with the totality of creative energy.

Dr. Stanislav Grof

I N EXPLORING THE PROFOUND INFLUENCE of the
birth process, Dr. Stanislav Grof talks about the
four stages we all go through during the womb-to-
world transition. He calls them BPMs or Basic Perinatal
Matrices. Briefly, BPM-1 refers to the heavenly bliss of
life in the womb where we feel safe and all our needs
are met. BPM-2 occurs when heaven turns to hell as
powerful forces begin crushing us, our environment
becomes toxic, and there's no hope of escape. BPM-3 is
when a narrow passage appears and we fight to make
the journey through it, and BPM-4 is physical birth
from womb to world.

According to Dr. Grof and others, the birth process is the most powerful and formative event we ever experience. According to me, what we call life is actually gestation. The womb-to-world transition is stage-one of a complete two-stage human birth process, but the second stage, transition from juvenile-to-adult, is not recognized as part of the process because it has been erased from the human experience.

Let's think about that for a minute: Our developmental spectrum runs the half-gamut from conception to childhood, leaving our adult development not just undiscovered but unsuspected. We presume to call ourselves bold pioneers of unexplored frontiers despite remaining totally ignorant of our own essential natures. We live and die as tiny acorns, never suspecting the mighty oaks that lurk within. If I'm wrong and humanity is currently at full development, then I'm just another ass-talker making outlandish claims, but if I'm right, then this is by far the most important observation in the history of mankind.

Just sayin'.

◈

Grof's stage-one birth matrices can also be applied to the belated stage-two rebirth process; the transition from the Segregated State of Human Childhood to the Integrated State of Human Adulthood. Instead of BPMs, Basic Perinatal Matrices, we can call the second-stage versions Belated Rebirth Matrices, or

BRMs. The word belated distinguishes this process from the on-time version of stage-two transition that would occur around the age of sexual maturity if it ever did, but it never does. We can reserve the term Peripubertal Rebirth Matrices as a placeholder in case anything changes on that front, but it never will.

BRM-1 is about life in the herdwomb; having all your needs met and being reliant on the dominant, superior organism of which you're a subservient, inferior part. BRM-2 begins, if ever, when the enfolding comfort, safety, and guidance of the herdwomb becomes a crushing, toxic hell with no hope of survival or escape. BRM-3 is the struggle through the rebirth canal of the black hole within, and BRM-4 is emergence into the Integrated State of Human Adult and the life of creative adventure that follows.

In short, the Belated Rebirth Matrices describe the one and only "spiritual" path. Any path that does not entail a death-rebirth transition into adulthood must necessarily result in remaining a halfborn, herdbound, eyes-closed, fear-based juvenile. Adulthood is not spiritual and it's not about enlightenment. It's not mystical or magical, it's just what humans are supposed to become but somehow don't. If anything, *not* achieving full and rightful development is the magical, mysterious thing, whereas adulthood is just our natural development.

❖

The BRM-1 version of the womb is the enclosing, enveloping, nourishing herd: Heaven. Go to school, get a job, have a family, grow old and die. Enter stage left, hit your marks, speak your lines, exit stage right. The path is as well-worn and easily followed as a cattle chute in an abattoir. You never have to worry or think or doubt or be alone, you just have to abdicate self-sovereignty and subordinate your will to that of the herdbeast, and for your reward, you can coast from cradle to grave without worrying your pretty little head about self-determination or self-realization. In the herd as in the womb, you can't see anything, you don't understand anything, and you can't make your own decisions except within the narrowest of confines, but that's a small price to pay for such a tidy answer to the messy question of how to dispose of a life you never asked for in the first place.

Belated Rebirth Matrix-2 parallels the stage-one womb event in which the ecstasies of the amniotic universe become the agonies of a poisonous, crushing, inescapable torment: Hell. In BRM-2, human childhood and life in the herd become unbearable, but there's nothing to do and nowhere to go. You are being crushed and poisoned and there's nothing you can do about it. You are trapped in a hopeless, no-escape, imminent-death scenario and behold, the way is closed unto thee.

BRM-3 begins when a way forward appears and you struggle toward it; a long journey of unbecoming that ends in the demise of the juvenile self: Death. The series of contractions and relaxations that can take a few hours in stage one can take a few years in stage two, but this time it's you giving birth to yourself.

BRM-3 ends with the step into the abyss which becomes the emergence stage of BRM-4, delivering us into our authentic fullborn state: Rebirth.

The journey to adulthood is not just another spiritual path, it's the one that looks exactly like the one that got you here in the first place. Heaven. Hell. Death. Rebirth; that's the only way forward. If you don't like the sound of that, I don't blame you; it sucks. It does make a strong case for meditation though; overlooking its ineffectiveness, it's easy to see why peace-and-silence (honey) would attract more followers (flies) than hell-and-death (vinegar). It's also easy to see why coming-of-age ceremonies are popular stand-ins for the actual process of transition, and why empty rites, false idols, and pseudo-sacraments have replaced authentic elements of the human experience.

❖

To put all this in *Joe vs the Volcano* terms, Belated Rebirth Matrix-1 is Joe at the beginning of the movie where he's still marching in lockstep with the herd; not happy, but not sufficiently unhappy to do anything about it. BRM-2 is initiated by a dire medical prognosis, but he's trapped in his circumstances and time is running out, so he just sits around and waits to die. BRM-3 is the journey that begins when Samuel Graynamore knocks on Joe's door and ends when Joe crosses the lip of the volcano. BRM-4 begins when Joe emerges into a new and superior state of being.

Without the intervention of demon/angel Samuel Graynamore, Joe would have spent the rest of his life with his exotic lamp and adventure books in his dungeonesque office. Graynamore is portrayed as an eccentric industrialist manipulating a poor schlub for his own greedy ends, but by his fruit shall we know him. It was Graynamore who had Dr. Ellison give Joe the false prognosis of a terminal "braincloud" that initiated Joe's shift to BRM-2. It was Graynamore who then appeared in person and opened Joe's way forward into and through BRM-3. Graynamore is the one who cut Joe's bonds, set his journey in motion and delivered Joe to the brink of a new life; Joe himself was mostly just a passenger. Graynamore never achieved his stated goal, but he did set Joe free. Graynamore may appear as a conniving demon, but judging by the fruit of his actions, he is Joe's liberating angel. That's how this stuff really works. False saviors ensure our continued imprisonment, while true liberators – falling somewhere on the spectrum between Graynamore and O'Brien – appear as malefactors and monsters. The trick with angels and demons is knowing which is which, but there's an easy way to tell the difference; the angels are the ones who are trying to kill you.

❖

The transition from BRM-1 to BRM-2 never comes from desire, goodness, evolution or growth, or any of the placebos, palliatives, and soporifics the pushers in the spiritual marketplace promote. BRM-2 begins when the comfortable herd environment suddenly becomes so toxic and crushing that death is imminent and there's nothing you can do and nowhere to run. This isn't just fanciful metaphor or poetic allegory, just as it wasn't fanciful or poetic when you went through it the first time; the original rude awakening. Don't remember? You were living in the warm bliss of the amniotic universe as your first experience of life, but it turned very bad very fast and there was nothing you could do about it. This actually happened to you. Imagine being comfortably asleep in your warm, safe bed in your highrise apartment when an earthquake hits like a freight train crashing through your bedroom. Imagine your building collapses and you're crushed beneath tons of rubble with only acrid black smoke to breathe and no hope of rescue or escape. Imagine that you're just a baby when that happens. Now stop imagining. You really went through that horrific shit, and just because you don't consciously remember it doesn't mean it didn't happen or that it wasn't the most profoundly influential event of your life.

Imagine a similar thing happening now. Imagine that your environment becomes so crushing and toxic that escape is impossible and death is imminent. One minute you're managing to keep up with your surrounding herdmates, and the next minute you're on the ground and there's nothing you can do but curl up and wait to be trampled to death by the larger organism of which you're no longer a part. That's what you can expect in stage two of your birth process, and somewhere inside you know it because you've already been through it. You may not consciously remember it, but you're hellbent on never going through it again.

❖

BRM-3 is the struggle for survival, and the result is something of a mixed bag. It begins when a ray of light appears through all those stomping hooves revealing, if not a path to safety, at least a direction of travel. It looks like an impossible struggle, but at least now there's action to be taken.

Ironically, the BRM-3 journey is not about survival but surrender; a long, slow crawl toward personal dissolution. Whatever you cling to during this process will be ripped away, whatever you hide will be found, whatever you extend will be cut off. It's not that you sever attachments, but that you slice off the parts of yourself that are attached. If thine eye offendeth thee, you don't sever your emotional attachment to it, you pluck it out and cast it from thee. As your ego-armor gets torn away, you become less attracted to the magnetic pull of the herd. The same forces that were crushing you are now expelling you.

Not to belabor the contraction/relaxation aspect of the delivery process, but it's another clear parallel. This journey is marked by surges of forward exertion followed by periods of rest and a buildup to the next surge. This cycle repeats again and again, each buildup and surge resulting in a single step, each step its own battle in a seemingly endless war.

Your journey continues until you reach the precipice where only one step remains; the last step of one life and the first step of another. It's at this point that you die from childhood and are born into adulthood, just as you once died from the womb and were born into childhood. BRM-2 is an ending and BRM-4 is a beginning, but BRM-3 is where the actual journey takes place; where the real war is fought.

◈

The further you travel from the heart of the herd, the colder and darker and lonelier it gets until you find yourself in a barren landscape devoid of human presence. You keep trudging along, one painful step at a time, when off in the distance you see the chimney smoke and warm, glow of a cabin. You knock on the door and are welcomed in by people who went their own way, just like you, who made it this far, just like you, driven by invisible forces, just like you. These are people who understand you and have answers for you, who will take you in and embrace you and tell you that you've finally arrived. You never dared to hope that such people actually existed, but now you've found them and you're one of them and you can be with them forever. Your gratitude and relief are inexpressible. Imagine how difficult it is then to realize that this place of comfort and camaraderie is just another temptation where you are once again confronted with the choice of melting back into a womb-like environment, or summoning all the power of will you can muster and going back out into the dark, frigid wasteland to continue a journey in which you not only have no hope of success, but that you're pretty sure is the stupidest thing anyone has ever done. That lonely trek into the barren wastelands of your dark interior is what the real spiritual journey looks like, and that's why so few ever awaken *in* the dreamstate, much less *from* it. The difference between those who settle into cabin life and those who keep going is their source of motivation. Ego, vanity, and the desire for bliss can only get you so far; the real journey is powered by a molten core burning within. Every time you stop in one of those lovely cabins to sit by the warm fire and enjoy the company, you have to stand back up, strap back into the cold steel of suicidal resolve, and head back out into the dark, lonely night.

Goddess VI:
The Mother of All Things

*Upon crossing the threshold, Bubby transforms
into a tall, radiant goddess in flowing silk robes.
Yin, Yang and Old Lady fall trembling to their
knees, heads pressed against the ground. Lao
Tzu remains seated.*

LAO TZU
Always with the big entrance.

YIN
We kneel before thee, mighty goddess!

YANG
We prostrate ourselves before your great magic!

OLD LADY
And terrifying beauty!

YANG

Oh yeah, and terrifying beauty!

GODDESS

Would you prefer my other face?

OLD LADY

I think we've seen it.

GODDESS

I have many faces. Arise. Stand and regard me.

Yin, Yang and Old Lady stand and keep their heads bowed.

GODDESS

to Lao Tzu

So, introduce me to your friends.

LAO TZU

Everybody, Goddess. Goddess, everybody.

GODDESS

Hi guys. Anything to eat around here?

LAO TZU

They were gonna eat *you.*

GODDESS

I'm something of an acquired taste.

LAO TZU

And a little hard to swallow.

GODDESS

Really people, nothing? A sandwich, a bag of chips?

to Lao Tzu

Why aren't you playing your part?

LAO TZU

You're the one who barged in here and broke character.

GODDESS

Lighten up, they had me tied to the pissing rock for four days. So what's the deal in here?

LAO TZU

Just banging out a bestseller.

OLD LADY

The Tao of the Large-Breasted Goddess with the Shapely Behind!

GODDESS

The Book of the Way will do fine. Have a seat, honey.

LAO TZU

I thought you weren't supposed to interfere.

GODDESS

I don't command, I suggest. At ease, boys. Just continue as if I wasn't here.

LAO TZU

Yeah guys, just continue as if a water buffalo didn't just walk into your shack and turn into a large-breasted goddess with a shapely behind who is now looking for some chips and asking about the book you're writing so you can live in pagodas by the sea. Nothing to see here.

GODDESS

Okay, so where are we? You've been writing? What have you got?

OLD LADY

Fortune cookie wisdom and gibberish.

GODDESS

A surefire recipe for success. We don't want to give away the good stuff.

YIN

clutching parchments

This isn't the good stuff?

GODDESS

I don't know what you have there, dear. I'm just a beast of burden. Tell me what you've written.

YIN

reads

If you want to weaken something, you must let it grow strong. If you want to eliminate something, you must let it flourish. This is called subtle illumination. Who knows how it will all end?

Is there no right and wrong? The sage is upright without causing harm, honest without hurting, illuminated but not flashy.

GODDESS

to Lao Tzu

Illuminated but not flashy?

LAO TZU

It's been a long four days.

YIN

reads

Without the body, what distress could there be? Only if you love your body as much as the world can you be entrusted with the world. Know the manly but cling to the womanly. Great-minded people abide in the kernel, not the husk.

GODDESS

to Lao Tzu

Really? This is what you've been doing while I was out there freezing my nosering off?

LAO TZU

You said...

GODDESS

I know what I said, mystical mumbo-jumbo, not amateur night at a comedy club.

OLD LADY

That's what I said! Fortune cookie wisdom and gibberish!

GODDESS

You've got the right idea, young lady. Why don't you try one?

OLD LADY

Me!? Oh, I couldn't.

GODDESS

Why not? You can't do any worse than Mr. Venerable over there. You've had four days to think about it. Just make an observation from your own life. You have kids, right? Speak from the heart.

OLD LADY

Uh, okay. The Tao is the mother of all things. Knowing the children is knowing the mother. Knowing both mother and children brings an end to fear. Oh, that was terrible!

GODDESS

That was great! A star is born! Try another.

OLD LADY

I can't think of anything. What should I say?

GODDESS

Doesn't matter. Talk about your life. How do you get home from here?

OLD LADY

If I have any sense I keep to the main road, my only fear is straying from it. Keeping to the main road is easy, but people like to get sidetracked. That was no good.

GODDESS

That was perfect. Pure gold. See? That's all there is to it. Mr. Yin, your turn. How do you feel about being stuck in this remote shack? Do you miss the world? From the heart.

YIN

Without looking through the window, you can see the way of things. Without going outside, you can know the whole world. The farther you go, the less you know.

GODDESS

Wonderful! Mr. Yang, your turn. Just let it out.

YANG

The cries of roosters and dogs can be heard by one another. Hold on to the fruit and not the flower. Those who praise victory relish manslaughter.

GODDESS

Splendid! The clever person hears of the Tao and practices it diligently. The average person hears of the Tao and gives it thought now and again, and the dull person hears of the Tao and laughs aloud. Hence it is said... Mr. Yin? Let 'er rip.

YIN

Opening the vent and completing the enterprise will make one helpless. Though there be boats and carriages, there is no occasion to ride in them. The more skills men possess, the more strange contrivances appear. There are various kinds of instruments, but let them not be used.

GODDESS

Well done! Mr. Yang?

YANG

Being the valley of the world, eternal virtue will be full in you and you return to the state of uncarved wood. Let people return to making knots on ropes instead of writing. When the Tao rules the world, proud stallions pull dung carts.

GODDESS

I like where this is going. Young lady?

OLD LADY

Seal the openings, shut the doors, dull the sharpness, untie the knots, dim the light, and become one with the dust. To bear the country's disgrace is to rule the shrines of soil and grain. Those who are obedient to the law will roll up their sleeves and make the disobedient obey. The best way to carve is not to split.

GODDESS

And you, Mr. Venerable?

Lao Tzu

I am a fool. I am confused. Others are clear and bright, but I am dim and weak. Others are sharp and clever, but I am dull and stupid.

Yang

Wow, wisdom is fun!

Goddess

Sure it is! Anyone can do it. Deep inside you already know this stuff. You don't need a venerable master or a goddess or a book.

Old Lady

We need a book to make us rich.

Goddess

You're already rich, you just don't know it. Seek not without for treasures that lie within.

Old Lady

Yeah, but seriously, I want to be rich. No more fortune cookie gibberish, we want the good stuff.

Goddess

You already have it. Three precious gifts to be prized above all are compassion, moderation and humility.

Old Lady

Bullshit! I'm up to my ass in compassion, moderation and humility and what good is it?

I don't want to find greatness in little things, I want to find greatness in a pagoda by the sea full of jewels and servants and some proper utensils instead of these goddamn chopsticks!

GODDESS

The Tao that *can* be told speaks of flow and obstruction, but the Tao that *can't* be told speaks of whence thou came and whither thou goest, of who and what and where you really are. Is this the Tao you wish to hear?

OLD LADY

If it's the one that makes us rich and happy.

GODDESS

Very well, I shall tell you the secret Tao. You asked for it. Prepare to have your socks knocked off. Ready?

OLD LADY

Hell yeah! Yin, write this down. Finally, we're getting to the good stuff. No more of this bullshit about water!

GODDESS

Let us speak of water!

OLD LADY

Goddammit!

GODDESS

All Water is One Water. All Essence is One Essence.

In the Essence of Water find the Secret of the Tao.
In the Secret of the Tao find the Truth of Man.

OLD LADY

Are you sure this is the good stuff?

GODDESS

Water falls from Heaven as rain
  and returns to Heaven as Essence.
The one becomes the many, the many become the one.
The story of Man is the many.
The truth of Man is the One.

OLD LADY

I'm not really feeling it.

LAO TZU

You're losing them. They like the non-doing stuff better.

GODDESS

That which water touches, water becomes.
Tea, piss, brine, honey, sap.
The drop of rain becomes the sweat of the worker,
  the blood of the soldier, the tears of the mother.
Thus it is said;
Man descends from Heaven and ascends to Essence.
Thus turns the wheel of creation;
Thus moves the motionless Tao;
Thus is revealed the story of You.

YIN

Oh gosh, is it Tuesday already? I just remembered,
I have this thing...

OLD LADY

Keep writing, maybe it gets better.

GODDESS

No two drops are the same.
None falls twice, none turn back.
None are lost, none go astray, none are forgotten.
None has come before. None will come again.

YIN

Not getting better.

OLD LADY

Yeah, I'm not getting a bestseller vibe.

YANG

And what about the little fish?

GODDESS

In this moment thou art man or woman,
 mother, soldier, worker, slave;
Behind these many masks resides the
 eternal, essential, impersonal One.
When your earthly sojourn is over,
 and your human form falls away,
Return thee to the Essence whence you sprang.

JED McKENNA

OLD LADY

Can we spice this up a bit? Stick in a chase scene
or some sex or something? Rain falls, becomes a
lot of stuff and evaporates. I mean, big whoop!

GODDESS

When the drop falls into the stream,
 can you show me the original drop?
When the stream becomes the river,
 can you show me the original stream?
When the river returns to the sea,
 can you show me the original river?
When the eternal has welcomed you home,
 can you show me your temporal face?

YIN

Temporal face? I'm not writing that.

GODDESS

In the dream of many lies the truth of one.
In the secret of the drop lies the truth of the sea.
In the heart of man shines the light of Essence.

YANG

Wow, wisdom is boring!

GODDESS

Soldier and sage, laundress and goddess,
In form, diverse. In Essence, one.
This is known by those who know,
 is felt by those who feel,
 is seen by those who see.
The Truth of the False.

The reality of the dream.
The One behind the Many.
The Tao behind the Tao.

YIN

Jesus, I think my ears are starting to bleed.

GODDESS

Of the One we are born, and to the One return.
The Tao of ten-thousand things can be spoken.
The Tao of Essence cannot be spoken.

YIN

That doesn't seem to be stopping you.

OLD LADY

Seriously, I was supposed to pick up the kids at
the rice paddy like three days ago...

GODDESS

The Tao contains time, enfolds space, embraces mind.
It flows from nothing, yet all things flow from it.
Raindrop and ocean are, in essence, One.
Mighty and meek are, in essence, One.
Creator and destroyer are, in essence, One.
Master and slave are...

OLD LADY

Yeah, yeah, master and slave are, in essence,
one. Got it. Okay everybody, let's have a big
guardshack round of applause for...

GODDESS

Thus may you understand your Earthly sojourn.
One is all and all is One.
The ten-thousand things pass in time.
Truth is Unity. Essence alone abides.
Thus is the Tao behind the Tao revealed…

YANG

Is there much more? I was thinking of sweeping up.

GODDESS

Oh, c'mon, people! Am I just talking to myself? Are you even listening to this? This is the good stuff!

LAO TZU

I think you lost them back at "Let us speak of water."

GODDESS

This is what you're asking for! The key to everything, the story of you! Who and what and where you really are! I even set it to *verse* for chrissakes!

LAO TZU

You shoulda warmed them up with a few jokes. They like knock-knocks.

GODDESS

I offer you truth and you reject it! Oh well, you can't say I didn't try. Pearls before swine. So you

211

tell me, what would you like to hear?

OLD LADY

Please show us the way! The happy way with champagne and caviar and pagodas by the sea

YIN

Yes! What must we do in order to become at one with the *happy* Tao?

YANG

Yeah, not the raindrop Tao with the blood and piss and all that.

GODDESS

Very well, have the way your own way. What exactly did you have in mind?

OLD LADY

Mind! *Aha!* Now we're getting to the good stuff. Yin, keep writing. Gorgeous Goddess, are you saying we should be more mindful?

GODDESS

Uh, yeah, sure. Be more mindful, whatever that means. Why not?

YIN

Should we sit for long periods with our eyes closed and our minds empty while silently repeating a meaningless sound?

JED MCKENNA

GODDESS

Yeah, good. Turn off your mind to become more mindful. That makes perfect sense.

YANG

Should we stand naked on one leg and smear ourselves in ash and smoke a lot of weed?

GODDESS

Sounds like a party.

OLD LADY

Should we sit in uncomfortable positions for long hours and ponder imponderables while a sadistic asshole hits us with a stick?

GODDESS

Whatever floats your boat.

YIN

Should we spend our time and energy grooming our reflection in the eyes of others to avoid turning our attention inward?

GODDESS

Is that a real thing? Fine, yeah. Do that.

YANG

Shall we renounce the real for the unreal? Embrace the synthetic over the authentic? Accept symbolic rites, hollow ceremonies and false sacraments as real, while forgetting the truth they represent?

GODDESS

Sure, sounds like a plan.

YIN

Shall we place a mask over our original face? Play two-dimensional characters and immerse ourselves in petty drama? Strut and fret our hour upon the stage like cackling hens while turning a blind eye to our boundless creative potential?

GODDESS

I see you've given this some thought.

OLD LADY

Shall we just go about our lives as if everything made perfect sense when we don't have the first asshair of a clue what's going on around here? Shall we just lie and pretend and play make-believe like children afraid of the dark? Shall we construct fortifications of lies and fear and crawl inside...

GODDESS

Okay, listen, I'm gonna stop you there. You guys seem to have a pretty good handle on this so I'll let you just hang out and brainstorm. No bad ideas, right? Me and the old man are just gonna ease on down the road, maybe hang a left and check out this Booty guy, see if he needs help polishing his message. That middle-of-the-road thing shows real promise.

Lao Tzu and Goddess stand and make their goodbyes. Upon crossing the threshold, Goddess transforms back into Bubby. Old lady and the guards step outside to watch them go.

YIN

It goes without saying that none of this ever happened.

YANG

What never happened?

YIN

Maybe we can still write the book and be rich and happy.

OLD LADY

It's already written. *The Tao Te Ching.* The goddess said it was just fine the way it is. We shouldn't change a thing.

Lao Tzu and Bubby stroll off into the sunset.

LAO TZU

I'm uncertain what just happened.

GODDESS

Uncertainty *is* what just happened. I've sent a message open to clear misinterpretation to weave a safe spell of confusion that will span the generations and assure that no one ever figures out who and what and where they really are.

LAO TZU

But you tried to be honest with them.

GODDESS

I always play fair, but they are impervious. In them, truth has no place to enter.

LAO TZU

But what about integrity and honesty? What about decency and righteousness? What about the divine spark in the individual?

BUBBY

Try to see the small picture here. Nothing is what it seems. It's right to be wrong and good to be evil. Sickness is healthy, suffering brings pleasure. Destruction is a creative act, death is the meaning of life. Awareness abhors a vacuum. The entire spectrum of appearance must be populated. It's not about the players, it's about the play.

LAO TZU

But then, how can anyone ever awaken to their divine potential?

BUBBY

That's just another drama, no one's stopping you. But if you wake everyone up, they'll revert to their natural state and nothing is duller than nature. Believe me, I'm doing us all a favor. It's better for everyone this way. I'm not a liberator or a jailer, I'm simply a producer of dramatic spectacle. The play's the thing, and the show must go on.

LAO TZU

I wish I'd brought a tennis ball.

BUBBY

I'm a goddess, not a dog.

LAO TZU

You're only a goddess in a writer's imagination.

BUBBY

You're only a writer in mine.

Yin, Yang and Old Lady watch as Lao Tzu and Bubby disappear into the setting sun. Returning to the shack, they find that the Goddess has left a huge mountain of shit – not entirely metaphorical – blocking their path.

THE END

The Tao of Pain

I know my words are weapons,
full of danger, full of death.

Walt Whitman

A POWERFULLY-BUILT YOUNG MAN named Zeke, in his early twenties and wearing a Texas A&M shirt, explains to me and those assembled that he has suffered for many years from a kind of "soul-level pain", and that he's the victim of anti-spiritual forces which have forged in him some bond of earthly attachment too powerful to break. He'd totally wake up if it were possible, he assures us, but alas, his circumstances are uniquely challenging and the way is not open unto to him. This type of creative rationalization is both common and effective. He has constructed an ego-flattering narrative around what amounts to nothing more than his own spiritual inertia; the tendency of an ass on a couch to stay on a couch.

Peace, happiness, compassion, and contentment have become synonymous with spiritual success. The goal of modern spirituality is not to escape *from* the dungeon but to make yourself comfortable *within* it. Many spiritual teachers seem to endorse this view by acting as buddies, counselors and life-coaches, dispensing fluffy love rather than the more effective but less popular tough love. If you're unhappy about some issue, whether it's a bad relationship or bad karma or a bad hair day, you just tell your spiritual mucky-muck about it and instead of hitting you with a stick or zapping you with a taser or simply being honest with you, they will help restore your sense of peace, happiness and serenity. Your relationship, karma and hair still suck, but now you've had a sip of sugary spiritual Kool-Aid, so it's okay. These teachers want you to be happy because they want to be liked and thumbs-upped. Me, not so much. I don't care about your drama or your happiness or your thumb. If anything, I'd like to see you go the other way. My wish for you, if I had one, would be that you become unhappier, that you spiral down into a mortal despair that reaches suicidal intensity. If I were personally invested in your transition, I would hope you achieve that level of burning discontent because only then will you address the underlying cause and not the superficial symptoms. Only then might you break out of self-imposed bondage instead of continuing as a single zombie in a vast undead horde.

❖

"As to your pain," I reply to the anguished young man, Zeke, in a way I hope is useful to all gathered, "it's a blessing if you can put it to good use. You can deny and distract from your pain in a million different ways, or you can go into the pain and see where it takes you. Until you do that, your pain makes you a victim and provides an excuse for inaction. Maybe your particular challenge is real, or maybe it's the same dynamic I've seen a thousand times before. I've seen people in hospices and prisons and wheelchairs who didn't make excuses for themselves, and here you are with every advantage – young, fit, clever, approaching an age where actual awakening is actually possible – but you're 4F because of flat feet. Rotten luck, dammit; no spiritual warfare for you.

"Maybe your spiritual solution-providers have confirmed your self-diagnosis, but what they should have told you is that this is ego's standard ploy; make excuses, justify failure, create new attachments, find a convincing reason to sit down, shut up and keep your eyes closed. Fear teams up with vanity so you wear failure like a crown. We spoke earlier, I know you're a bright guy; educated, sincere, tenacious. I'm not trying to insult you. On the contrary, I see you as a particularly viable candidate for transition to adulthood, but before that can happen you have to achieve full-frontal death-awareness. That's where the unthinkable becomes the inevitable, where your polarity reverses and you're drawn toward a future that currently repels you. Until we open our eyes and see who and what and where we are, we'll never have an informed understanding of our situation and no forward progress will be possible. Once we open our eyes and see our situation clearly, all the ties that bind us to this juvenile identity dissolve and the way forward opens up. It's not fate or karma or luck, it's a journey of small steps, each one its own journey. You feel paralyzed because you're looking ahead when you should be focusing on the next step. It's like walking a tightrope; the trick is to take it nice and easy, one step at a time, and try not to look down."

I address myself to the whole group.

"I assume you're all experiencing some pain or discomfort or sense of unease. You didn't come here because you're perfectly happy with your current spiritual roadmap. Something's wrong. You feel it even if you can't describe it, a splinter in your mind, a not-rightness; a disconcerting sense that something is missing or wrong. That's the Little Bastard's voice getting through to you. I'm not a healer or a counselor or a guru, I don't love you any more or less than I love yon apple tree, but here you are anyway, which suggests that you're interested in going into those dark interior spaces and lighting them up; not that you *want* to, but that it hurts *not* to. Unlike your spiritual solution-providers however, I don't want to relieve your pain, I want to make it hurt more. The spiritual marketplace is all about easing or denying or ignoring your pain, but I want your pain to get worse, a *lot* worse. This is my wish for you."

Several of those assembled respond with nervous laughter; hoping I'm joking, worried I'm not.

"I'm not talking about a sense of mild despair that descends on you now and then – existential gloom or psycho-spiritual malaise – I'm talking about being radically misaligned with your own nature. You're all casualties of a war you didn't know you were fighting. A bomb went off in your life and left you shell-shocked and incoherent, and now you're laying in a hospitable bed hallucinating your life instead of out in the world living it. I am visiting your bedside, whispering in your ear. Are my words reaching you? Are you doing all you can to hear them? Do you even want to? Or are you happy enough living behind closed eyes?

"Suffering is a healthy sign that something is wrong, that you're violating the natural order of your being. That's how your spirit tells you something's not right, that *you're* not right. You run to the bookstore and the internet, to clergy and gurus, organizations and systems, distractions and addictions, to the mall or the stadium, to screens and hobbies, all in an attempt to reduce your spiritual dissonance by lubricating the contact surfaces where abrasion occurs. Meanwhile, the underlying cause goes undetected and is left to eat away at you like a cancer.

"Maybe you don't recognize this pain. Maybe you're just looking for a nice spiritual experience and you don't want to burn your life down to find it. If that applies to you, then you're in the wrong place listening to the wrong guy. I have no consolation prize to offer, no path to bliss, no technique for opening your third eye or raising your kundalini. All I have is the nuclear option, but why resort to that when all you want is a better night's sleep or increased mental clarity or the answers to a few nagging questions?

"What if I had an energetic technique that could totally heal your pain in one session? So what? Pain is not the problem, cancer is not the problem, mortality and loneliness are not the problems, they're just symptoms of the one true problem which is being trapped in the halfborn state. Are you unhappy? Are you suffering? Good, you should be. Your pain is telling you something is wrong and you should listen to it. I'm not here to end your pain. I agree with it. You *should* be uncomfortable, something *is* wrong. What could be more wrong than being trapped in the womb beyond your due date and thinking it's normal? You believe you're a fully developed being, that your eyes are open and you see things as they are, but your eyes are not open and your development has been prematurely terminated. Incomplete emergence is the one cause and everything else is just an effect. Nothing you do matters and you're going to die, so what's not to be unhappy about? You are perfectly justified to be in pain, the more the better, but don't waste your lifeforce denying it or addressing symptoms, go after the cause. *If man will strike, strike through the mask! How can the prisoner reach outside except by thrusting through the wall?* Go into the pain, go into the fear; they're like beacons guiding you inward. Get in there and find out what's going on. Use the process of spiritual autolysis to find your way. Truth doesn't hurt, lies do. Your pain doesn't come from the fact that your life is meaningless and you're going to die, it comes from pretending your life has meaning and that you're going to live forever. It comes from living a bullshit life. It doesn't come from the truth of no-self but the illusion of self; not from the unknown but from fear and denial of the unknown. I myself am awake both in and from the dreamstate but I don't get a special pass; my life is still meaningless and I'm still going to die. That doesn't cause me any discomfort because I don't pretend my life is something it's not; namely, mine. My death is my one true friend. It walks before me in the light, not behind me in the shadows. I am always aware of it so I never forget who and what and where I am.

"Fear weaponizes your imagination against you, but some remote corner of your brain is still uninfected and it's telling you that all your soothing notions of heaven, reincarnation and immortality are just an excuse for sitting on the couch. Ego tricks you into believing that there is no urgency, but the game has started and the clock is running. Your whole life is a constant effort not to fall through the rickety trapdoor you know you're standing on but pretend you're not. It's a delicate balancing act; one false move and you could be plunged into the darkness you've spent your life avoiding. It's like treading water; you can never stop or you'll sink like a rock, but sinking into that inky blackness is the one and only spiritual path.

"The real problem isn't that you're *unhappy* but that you're not unhappy *enough*. You're not suffering enough. Your discontent has not reached an actionable level. Think of Joe working in that dungeon-like office. If it hadn't been for the intervention of demon-angel Graynamore, Joe would have spent the rest of his life in mindless drudgery. Graynamore chose Joe because he had a spark in him; the courage he displayed during his time as a firefighter. You have that spark too; we know that because you're here. It's buried somewhere inside you and that's where it will die if you don't uncover it and coax it back to life."

I pause and take a drink of bottled water. I rub my hands at the fire and remind myself as I do, many times a day, how awesome hands are and how nice it is to have a body to attach them to and a dreamstate to keep them in. And that I won't have them forever.

"So let's say I actually had a cure for all pain. So what? I'd get rich and famous. They'd give me my own magazine and talk show. I'd have my own airplane, my own entourage, my own little empire. I'd wear big gem-encrusted eyeglasses and spiky hair-mousse and a zany bow tie so everyone would know how whacky-wise I am while I peddle my pain solution on the talkshow and booksigning circuit, and everyone would line up to pay. But again, so what? Maybe in a dungeon being pain-free is the best we can do, but why stay in a dungeon when we're free to leave? That's what you're asking by being here, and this is the answer. The cure for all suffering is to go into it. Pain is your friend, your guiding light. It's there for your benefit. Stop denying, medicating and spiritualizing your way out of it and start fighting your way into it. If you're out of alignment, pain is natural, but instead of fixing the alignment we address the pain. Your pain stems from your resistance to your own development, so if you want to end your pain, you have to find your inner black hole, dig it out from under whatever garbage dump of emotional debris you've piled over it, and crawl into it.

"If I could create a technique to end everyone's suffering, I wouldn't do it. Your pain is your perfect intelligence sending you a message, but you're drowning it out with emotional static. You spend your time and lifeforce running up the down escalator, but if you stop fighting and let it carry you into those shadowy depths, you can start looking for your authentic life. The way up is down, the way out is through, and that act of surrender, that trustfall into the void, is the difference between success and failure on the spiritual journey."

⬦

"When I look at you guys, I wonder what you might become if you grew into your potential; about the better versions of yourselves you'd discover if you'd trust the universe to show you; what kind of tree you might become, what unique fruit might you bear. I look at you guys and it seems like you feel guilty of some unspecified crime, like Josef K. in Kafka's *The Trial*, like you don't belong here, like you're trespassing on someone else's property or committing some crime just by existing. I think the reason I see that in you is that I remember it about me, but I've forgotten what it's like to feel that way. My sense of self has expanded to encompass all I behold. I don't end where my skin ends but where my sight and hearing and feeling end, where my awareness ends; at the outer limits of my thoughts and feelings and imagination. I'm not *in* my dreamstate, I *am* my dreamstate. A better way to express no-self is *all*-self. It's not that there's *no* me but that it's *all* me. I guess that's what they mean by unity consciousness, but it doesn't seem special or elevated, it's just natural and normal and people who aren't this way seem like placeholders for their actual selves who have yet to arrive. That's what I think when I look at you guys. I'm waiting for you to show up. I don't know what's keeping you, but I look forward to meeting you.

"I myself am an open book. My spiritual DNA is open-source; when you read my writings you read my code. You understand me as well as I understand myself because all I am is in the books. They are the ship's logs of my ongoing journey. I am fixed on an outbound course and the only person who will ever be further out on my trajectory is future-me. There's a different trajectory awaiting each of us; the question is, what's yours? Why aren't you out here seeing what I see and showing me what you see? Why aren't you already a million miles high and climbing? Why aren't you so far gone that you laugh to recall you once identified as human? This body is not what you are, it's a launch platform for what you might become, but here you are playing a background character on this shabby little stage while your unique potential goes unexplored and unexpressed. Think of how McMurphy in *Cuckoo's Nest* freaked out when he learned that his fellow inmates were voluntarily incarcerated and could leave whenever they wanted. That's how I feel when I look at you. You're asking me what life is like outside the cuckoo's nest when all you have to do is go see for yourself; strike through the mask, thrust through the wall like Chief Broom and emerge into whatever lies beyond. Even if he was killed by police five minutes later, the Chief still won. Just like Captain Ahab, his victory was absolute.

"Your inner black hole is like a sucking chestwound. You spend your life denying it, ashamed of it, covering it up, decorating it, accessorizing it, pretending it's not there, that it's something else, that it's okay because everyone has one. You bandage it to hide it, smear it with ointments to soothe it, take drugs for the pain. You have remedies to help you forget it and techniques to distract you from it, but it's always there, a black hole at the very heart of your being. Spirituality and religion exist to help you pretend it's not there and mask the pain, but I'm suggesting that you go the other way. Tear open your shirt, rip off the bandage, wipe off the ointment, get off the drugs and deal with the black wound. Face it, feel the pain. Look *at* the wound and *in*to it. If it doesn't hurt enough, make it hurt more; punch it, stab it, wake it up. Right now you're here with me, listening to words that are not meant to soothe but are meant to hurt, and you're not running away, so maybe the process has begun for you. Maybe you can go home to your kitchen table and pick up a pen and start probing that wound for yourself. And the thing you should know, the thing you're not expecting, is that as you start digging *in* from the *out*side, another part of you starts digging *out* from the *in*side, and when those two parts unite, the process will take on a life of its own and there will be no stopping it. That's how it works and there is no other way."

❖

Going into the fear and pain is the only road to salvation there is and I seem to be the only one talking about it, so where does that leave us? Are you ready to

become a Jedvaitin or join the Church of Aletheology
and accept me as your personal savior? Gosh, that's a
scary thought; I barely accept me as my personal dog
walker, but I guess we have to play the hand we're
dealt. I don't keep close tabs on all the gurus out
there, but based on individual results and the state
of modern spirituality as a whole, I'd say that our
spiritual solution-providers might be the problem that
needs solving, so, as wonky-doodle as it sounds, like
some dark knight on a quest to rid the world of spiritual villainy and usher in a new age of enlightenment,
Sri Sri Sri Sri Jed may not be the savior we deserve, but
he *is* the savior we need. And I'm sure it goes without
saying, but just in case there's any question, an enclosed
cab with climate control would be simply divine. Oh,
did I mention surround sound? That would be pretty
sweet. I mean, unless, you know, you don't feel that
humanity's in-life savior should be able to crank some
tunes while he works. That's fine, that's cool, whatever.
It's just a minor add-on, but hey, if it's too much...
Well, give it some thought, but please guys, let's not
skimp on the backup camera and 360-degree lighting
system. I'm sure our in-life savior would like to see
where he's going, especially when he's running that
big-ass brush grinder. Oh, did I mention the big-ass
brush grinder? I bet our guy would love one of those.
I know I would.

Mystery Prize

Promise me you'll always remember: You're braver
than you believe, and stronger than you seem, and
smarter than you think.

Christopher Robin to Winnie-the-Pooh

YOU'RE A CONTESTANT ON *Let's Make A Deal*,
jumping up and down in a chickensuit holding
up a sign that says "Me Me! Me!" You've already won
a nice set of cookware valued at over four hundred
dollars, but now, host Bob is asking if you want to
trade your space-age cookware for what's behind door
number two. What do you do? The future is a darkness into which none can peer but all must step. Does
your future lie ahead or behind? Forward or back? Do
you take your cookware and walk away, or risk it all
for your big shot at the mystery prize?

It's an easy decision when you're bouncing up and down on your couch yelling at the TV, but now it's *you* jumping up and down, now it's *your* cookware at stake, and now Bob wants an answer. What do you do? Take your cookware and quit, or keep playing?

We can bring this analogy into focus with a few minor adjustments. Instead of cookware, you're playing for everything – family, friends, fortune, future – your entire life. Instead of a ridiculous chickensuit, you're wearing a ridiculous humansuit. Instead of wondering if there's a grand prize or a booby prize behind the curtain, you're wondering if it's a new life or no life at all, and instead of all this happening hypothetically, it's happening right now. Bob is the Little Bastard within, this is the game of life, and you're playing right now whether you know it or not, want to or not, like it or not.

Bob needs an answer and here's the answer you're going to give: "I think I'll just take my cookware and go home, Bob." And Bob will frown and ask, "Are you sure? You don't get an offer like this every day!" And you'll pretend to struggle with temptation, but you'll say, "Yes Bob, I don't want to go any further, I want to stop. Final answer." The audience will be disappointed, but they'll applaud when the sign tells them to because they want to be applauded when they make the same decision.

The promise of the spiritual marketplace is that you can have your cookware *and* what's behind the mystery curtain, and what's behind the curtain is beyond your dreams. That's the golden lie underpinning all spirituality, as billions of sincere, intelligent seekers who spent their lives jumping up and down in chickensuits and kneeling at the shrine of consolation cookware can tell you.

Confronted with a choice between consolation prize and mystery prize, we'll always take the cookware. Stepping into the volcano is not about faith or desire or willpower because it's never presented as an option; it's what remains when options have disappeared. That wonderful cookware represents contentment in captivity; as long as you have a home and family and a life to take your cookware back to, that's what you'll choose to do. We never step into the abyss out of faith or desire or strength of will, we only do it because the path behind us has disappeared and the ground beneath us is crumbling. That's where *Joe Versus the Volcano* deceives us. Joe would never have jumped. He would have gone off with Patricia and they would have gotten properly married. They would have bought a condo in Waikiki, opened a trendy bistro, and had a couple of kids who wonder why Grandpa Sam never comes to visit.

None of the reasons that make sense getting to the volcano still make sense when you're standing on the edge looking down into a raging torrent of final dissolution. It's never a choice because all choices were made back in the first spark of this slow-motion explosion.

None of those steps that got you here were made voluntarily, and the last one is no different. If he'd had a choice, Joe would have taken his consolation bride back to a better cell in the same prison, and rejoined a herd he never really left.

In the acorn slumbers the mighty oak. The full expression of Joe was in his spiritual DNA all along, just waiting for an environment conducive to his emergence, just as your spiritual DNA sits dormant inside you, waiting for conditions to be right. Is it still viable? Is emergence still possible?

Maybe.

Don't worry about the future, just focus on the next step. If it feels like you're tumbling in freefall, just remember to trust the arch; chest forward, facing into the fall, eyes open, totally in control despite being totally out of control. That's how you turn a bad situation around. That's how you knock Bob on his ass and send the crappy cookware flying and tear down the goddamn curtain. That's how you find out who and what and where you really are.

Wisefool Press

STAKE LIFE UPON TRUTH

Visit Wisefool Press to find out more about Jed's books. Be sure to sign up for free articles and notifications, download the free ebook *Thus Spake Jed McKenna* and other free content, and see the collection of spiritual quotations and gallery.

WWW.WISEFOOLPRESS.COM

www.ingramcontent.com/pod-product-compliance
Lightning Source LLC
Chambersburg PA
CBHW072136090426
42739CB00013B/3210